8 Trips to Heaven

Encounters With God the Father
and the Lord Jesus Christ

"One of the things that have affected Christianity as a whole, and the Church, in particular, are unanswered questions that relate to the Person or Deity of the Lord Jesus Christ."

UNVEILING THE HIDDEN TRUTH ABOUT JESUS CHRIST

This book is a Gift

from

....

to

....

on the occasion of

....

date

....

May this book stir up a longing in your heart to know Jesus Christ more, and build a lasting relationship with God the Father through Him. Amen!

8 Trips to Heaven

Encounters with God the Father and the Lord Jesus Christ

The True Testimony of Evangelist

PIERRE M. NORAME

8 TRIPS TO HEAVEN: *Encounters with God the Father and the Lord Jesus Christ: Unveiling the Hidden Truth About Jesus Christ*

Copyright © 2021 by **Pierre M. Norame**

ISBN: 978-978-55441-2-1

Published by:

KINGS VIEW PUBLISHING HOUSE
Calabar, Nigeria/ Tbilisi, Georgia
www.kingsviewbooks.com
E-mail: enquiries@kingsviewbooks.com
+995 568 286 737; +2347035358454

All Scripture quotations are taken from the Authorised King James version and The New King James Version of The Holy Bible, except otherwise indicated.

For further information, please contact:

Evang. Pierre M. Norame

401 WEST LANTANA ROAD SUITE 10
LANTANA FLORIDA 33462
+1(561)410-6536
Pnoramebooks@hitaj.org
www.hitaj.org

Printed in the United States of America

"I am a child of God just like any other believer. All I describe in this book are privileges that I have been granted by the grace of God, not because of any special merit. And this privilege doesn't make me greater than you in any way. I'll like you to have this at the back of your mind while going through this book."

Dedication

To my Lord and Savior,

Jesus Christ

Whose Love has turned my life around and made
something out of nothing.

Preface

TO THE INTERNATIONAL EDITION

If anyone comes to me and does not hate father and mother, wife and children, brothers and sisters—yes, even their own life—such a person cannot be my disciple.

Luke 14:26

Before I start explaining my trips to Heaven and the times that I've seen God the Father and the Lord Jesus Christ, I think it's best to tell you how it started.

It's been six years since my ex-wife and I have been

separated, and now divorced. But what I love about the grace of God is that, until today, no woman can accuse me of an immoral affair with them.

Has it been easy in the flesh not to have an affair with anyone in those many years? Of course not, but the Lord took advantage of my wife's leaving, to prepare me for the special journeys He granted me in His mercies.

I remember when my wife left me in May 2015, I wanted to harm myself because I felt like life was over for me. That was because I loved her so much. Was there anything wrong with loving my wife? No, of course. But there was something more to it.

The Lord Jesus taught us in Luke 14:26, *If anyone comes to me and does not hate father and mother, wife and children, brothers and sisters—yes, even their own life—such a person cannot be my disciple.*

Well, I was one of those men who loved their wives even more than the Lord. This was quite subtle, and I didn't notice it until I found myself in that situation. I was so addicted to having great moments with my wife that I kept asking God how I could stay without her for days. It was tough, and I thought it would be impossible.

But here I am, six years after.

This tells me that we don't really know ourselves at all. We always think we can't cope under certain conditions. But it's so true that we can do all things with the Lord on our side. Without Him, we can do nothing.

The Apostle Paul said in Philippians 4:13, *I can do all things through Christ which strengtheneth me.* And our Lord Jesus said, *for without me ye can do nothing* (John 15:5).

Both Scriptures point to the same thing: With Christ, we can do all things; without Him, we can do nothing. So, if you're in Christ, of course, you can do all things if it pleases the Father.

That experience opened me up to love the Lord

even more, and live to please Him every day of my life. This became a foundation for the incredible privileges the Lord would later grant in my life, which have given birth to this book.

Pierre M. Norame
Florida, USA
June 2021

Introduction

T his book is all about my Eight Trips to Heaven, the six times I've seen God the Father, the thirteen times I've seen the Lord Jesus Christ, and that one time I heard God's voice talking to me clearly.

So, in this book, I will be sharing all my experiences with God the Father, and the Lord Jesus Christ.

I will also be sharing what I call the Hidden Truth about Jesus Christ. That is, everything I was taught by God the Father Who revealed to me Who Christ Jesus really is - His Living Word, God Himself, the Eternal One Who was, is, and will be living forever with God the Father as His only Perfect Word.

One of the things that have affected Christianity as a whole, and the Church, in particular, are unanswered questions that relate to the Person or Deity of the Lord Jesus Christ. This alone has given rise to several sects, each believing that what they hold as true is the right thing.

This uncharted territory, by God's special mercies, will be addressed in this series. In my visits to Heaven, God revealed many of these things to me and I'll be sharing them accordingly.

I'm sure you may have an idea about some of these questions. Nevertheless, I've listed below a good number of those I'll be addressing in the next books in the series, based on the revelations given to me by God the Father.

1) *Who really is Jesus Christ?*
2) *Is Jesus Christ God the Father?*
3) *Did Jesus Christ claim to be God the Father?*
4) *If Jesus Christ is God (YHWH), how come He was always praying to the Father?*
5) *When Jesus Christ was on earth, was He inferior to*

God the Father?

6) When Jesus Christ said in John 14:28, 'My Father is greater than I,' what did He mean? Is that actually so today?

7) If Jesus Christ is God the Father, then why did He say in John 5:19, 'the Son can do nothing of Himself?'

8) If Jesus Christ is the First born of all creation according to Colossians 1:15, how come He is God the Father who is Eternal?

9) Some people claim that Jesus Christ was created according to Proverbs 8:22-31. Is this true?

10) Who created the Universe? God the Father or Jesus Christ?

11) Does God the Father have the form of a human being?

12) When Jesus Christ said, 'Seek first the Kingdom,' what did He really say to seek?

13) When God (YHWH) talked about resting on a day, was He really talking about resting on a day?

14) When Jesus Christ said, 'No one knows about that day or hour, not even the Son, but only the Father,' does Jesus Christ not know the date or hour until today?

15) When Jesus Christ said in John 14:3-14, 'I will do whatever you ask in my Name,' what did He really mean by that?

16) How can someone truly love God, YHWH?

17) Do our prayers reach God the Spirit? If not, why? Or who stops them?

18) Did you know that Jesus Christ accepted to be our Custodian?

19) How come Jesus is God and our Advocate? Are they two different people?

20) If Jesus Christ is God, then why did the Apostle Paul say in 1Corinthians 11:3, 'The Head of Christ is God?'

21) Who will judge the World? Jesus Christ or God the Father? Matthew 25:31-33.

22) Why did God (YHWH) ask for all men to be circumcised in Genesis 17:9-14?

23) Why doesn't God (YHWH) forgive angels but mankind?

24) Was Jesus Christ against God's Word when He didn't condemn the adulterous woman in John 8:11, meanwhile, God Himself allowed anyone who committed adultery among His people to be stoned to death (Leviticus 20)?

25) Why did God (YHWH) give mankind marriage?

26) Why did God (YHWH) create sex for mankind?

27) Why doesn't God (YHWH) want anyone to have sex before marriage?

28) Why is God (YHWH) against Homosexuality?

29) Will the true Church be going through the great tribulation?

30) Will mankind worship God (YHWH) forever in the New Earth?

You will agree with me that these are questions that have bothered the Church for ages, and have remained unanswered in many ways, even though many sects have been formed because of diverse opinions and beliefs. Nevertheless, God has been gracious enough to reveal these things to me, which I now share throughout this series.

I am sure this book will build up your faith in the Lord Jesus Christ the same as when you read about Moses, Abraham, the Prophet Isaiah, the Disciples of Jesus, and many other people who have encountered God in their visions and dreams, and several other ways.

Now, I want to quickly address an important concern. When people hear about someone who has been given the privilege of experiencing Heaven, God the Father, or the Lord Jesus Christ, they tend to think of them in very special ways. Sometimes, they accord them such a high honor that makes them think they're really better than others.

This is not right. I want you to know that no one is better than you in any way.

Yes, it's a great thing to go to Heaven or experience God the Father and the Lord Jesus Christ. It's a great and exciting feeling, but that doesn't place us on a higher pedestal than others. This is something we have to be careful about.

I am a child of God just like any other believer. All I describe in this book are privileges that I have been granted by the grace of God, not because of any special merit. And this privilege doesn't make me greater than you in any way. I'll like you to have this at the back of your mind while going through this book.

That said, I'll implore you to read this book with an open mind, expecting God to speak to you in a way that applies to your life and relationship with Him.

Do not approach this as another tale you'd want to garner information about, but an opportunity to grow in grace and the knowledge of God and the Lord Jesus Christ.

Shalom!

One

Head-to-Head
With God's
Purpose

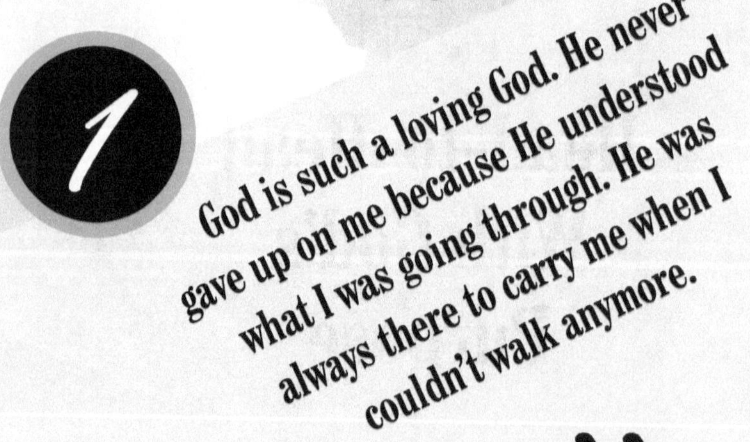

PURPOSE

1

"God is such a loving God. He never gave up on me because He understood what I was going through. He was always there to carry me when I couldn't walk anymore."

HEAD-TO-HEAD WITH GOD'S PURPOSE

> **On the sixth day, God called me up to Heaven. When I got there, I saw Him sit...**

About four to five months after my marital disharmony, I couldn't help but keep crying to God to have my wife come back to me.

All my prayers to God were only to have her come back home. That was how much I loved her. It is apparent that I loved her more than Christ, but I never realized it until God showed that to me. But the truth is, I was not ready to listen to anything God was telling me to do. I never opened my heart for God to speak with me at all. It was all about having her back to me.

If God tried to speak to me, I wouldn't care at that time because the wound was still fresh, and I cared less about anything else, except to have my wife back.

But God is such a loving God. He never gave up on me, because He understood what I was going through. He was always there to carry me when I couldn't walk anymore; where the road seemed to have ended for me.

He carried me through the dark. He carried me where there was nowhere to put my feet and walk on. He carried me through the rivers and fires, and even fought the devil and all of his demons on my behalf many times (I have explained these in a different chapter).

God the Father is a merciful God. He had a lot of patience with me.

I had my cousin come from Haiti at that time, because I was going through so much. She was a

Seventh-Day Adventist. She told me to fast and pray for seven days straight, to do 7 prayers, read 7 Psalms, and sing 7 songs every day for 7 days. They call it *Seven Tours of Jericho*.

Like I said, I was doing everything people would tell me to do to have my wife back because all I ever needed at that time was for her to come back. So, I started fasting.

On the sixth (6th) day, God called me up to Heaven. When I got there, I saw Him sit down on His Throne and had an angel standing on the left side of the Throne.

I didn't know the reason why God called me up to come to Him. I thought it was good news that He heard my prayers. But He spoke to the angel with an angry voice. I could see how unhappy He was when talking to the angel.

He said to him, "Isn't that his wife he needs? Go get him his wife, and he will see what's going to happen to him when she comes back to him."

God was yelling and commanding the angel to go get her to me. But He didn't say anything to me. On that trip, He was super furious.

When I woke up to start my 6th day of the Tour of

Jericho, I was so afraid, especially because of the revelation I had. So, that morning, instead of continuing to pray for my wife to come back, I completely turned around and was begging God to keep her away.

I said, "God you know I didn't know any better. You have to teach me Your ways. Please don't let her come back. Don't listen to my wicked heart praying to You. It wasn't my fault. Please God don't let her come to me. I'm so sorry for praying to You all of these crazy prayers from my flesh."

After that, I was so afraid, and I kept asking God to forgive me. I was hoping that she doesn't come back, because I was in deep trouble with God.

Also, I didn't know if God would listen to my prayers to keep her away from me. But I was just hoping, because I knew for sure if she came back, I would probably be dead.

I'm not saying that she was going to do anything wrong to me; only God knows that. But I'm sure that He wouldn't be with me anymore. I would be on my own. But I thank God that He listened and forgave me, and helped me to walk heart-to-heart with His purpose for my life.

And you know, even after all of that, I was still trying to make her come back after a few months passed. But this time, I was always asking God for His will to be done. And when I finally gave up completely, was after she divorced me.

I said to myself, that's it! I won't ever bother her anymore. I'll finally go pray to God to send me someone that He has well-prepared for me; someone that was made for me, born for me, and was God's choice for me.

I thank God that He listened and forgave me, and helped me to walk heart-to-heart with His purpose for my life.

Letting Go!

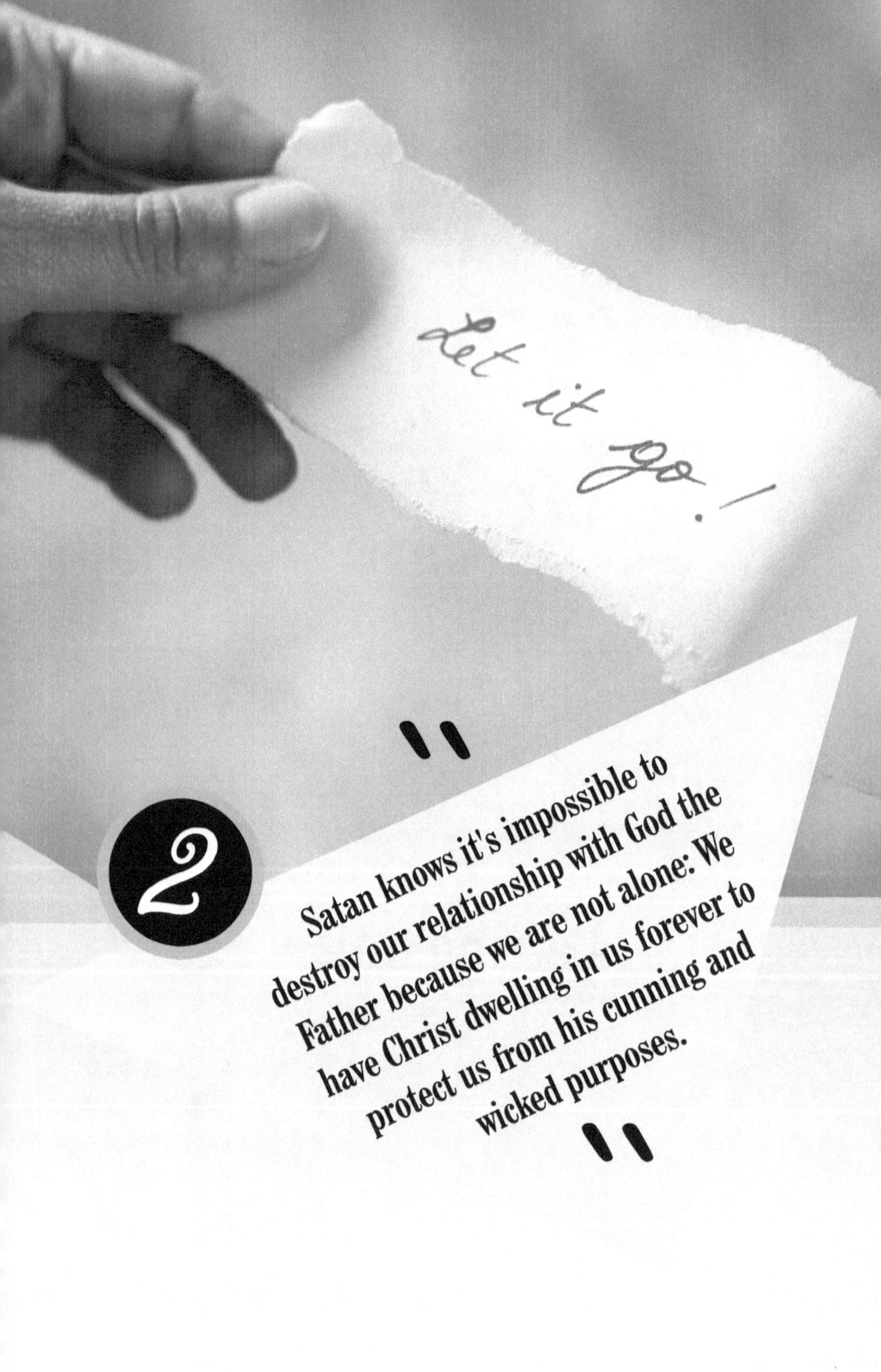
Let it go!

2

Satan knows it's impossible to destroy our relationship with God the Father because we are not alone: We have Christ dwelling in us forever to protect us from his cunning and wicked purposes.

Letting Go!

I strongly believe the devil broke my marriage so he could see if I was going to give up on God. And I can say that if it were for me, I would definitely give up on God, even before my marriage was broken. Yet, God took advantage of my situation and prepared me for who I am today in Christ.

The devil will always try as hard as he can to destroy our relationship with God the Father like he did with Adam and Eve by causing them to sin against God. It wasn't their fault, and there was no way they could avoid sin when satan was on earth with them, even though they were in a perfect body.

Now, Satan knows it's impossible to destroy our relationship with God the Father because we are not alone: We have Christ dwelling in us forever to protect us from his cunning and wicked purposes.

I can't thank God enough for letting the devil break my marriage. It's not like I wasn't happy with my marriage. Of course yes, I enjoyed my marriage. I loved my wife dearly. But sometimes, God allows certain things to happen to your marriage in order to make you enjoy something more precious than that.

Who knows why God allows certain things to happen to those He loves? Deuteronomy 29:29 says, "The secret things belong to the LORD our God." I don't need to question God about my situation because I know if He wanted, He could fix it.

One thing I know is that God will not change your spouse or anyone for you. It's not because He is unable to do it; He can. If it's in His will for His Name to be glorified, then you will surely benefit from it.

God's Word (Jesus Christ), which is the light of the World, will not be in compromise with the darkness. These two don't tie together. It's either the darkness comes to the light to become light as well if it's God's will, or the darkness separates itself from the light. Or, they both remain who they are, "light and darkness," separately. For instance, daytime and nighttime never meet.

That means, there is not much of a chance for a Christian and a non-Christian spouse to stay together in a relationship, unless God will bring the non-Christian spouse to the light.

If you are already married to a non-Christian spouse, I'm not saying he/she will not stay with you. In fact, here is what the great Apostle Paul wrote in 1Corinthians 7:16, *For how do you know, O wife, whether you will save your husband? Or how do you know, O husband, whether you will save your wife?*

Again, when I said, "the darkness separates itself from the light," the fifteenth verse makes it clear:

But if the unbeliever (darkness) departs, let him depart; a brother or a sister is not under bondage in such cases. But God has called us to peace.

I remember when Christ Jesus appeared to me in a revelation of the night. At that time, I lived on the second floor of the building. In that revelation, I saw that my ex-wife lived on the first floor, right under my unit.

I saw that she opened the door to talk to me, and her door was a right-hand/outswing.

While I was talking to her, she had no idea that Christ was coming behind her door. We were about twenty-five feet away talking to each other, but since I was facing her while talking, I was able to see Jesus Christ coming behind her door.

I don't think Jesus was coming to talk to her for me. I think He was rather coming to rebuke me, instead. I believe He is Omniscient and already knew that she was not going to let Him talk to her anyways.

When she noticed that I was focused on something that was coming from behind her door, she swung her head behind the door and saw Christ. And she recognized Him as Jesus

Christ. Once she saw Him, she slammed her door and shut it.

I said, "Jesus! What did she just do? Why did you let her shut the door on You and You didn't say anything? Don't you want her to come back to me?"

He said to me, "LEAVE HER."

I said, "What do you mean 'Leave her?'"

Then, He didn't say anything else to me.

And, He disappeared.

I ran down to see if she would open the door for me to talk to her, since Jesus didn't even try to knock on the door or say a word to her for me. But she wouldn't open the door for me.

When I looked through her front windows, I saw that her house was completely empty. There was no furniture there at all.

Maybe this could possibly mean a lack of Christ in her heart.

I pray God the Father heartily to send His Word (Christ) to go after that particularly wounded sheep to put her on His shoulders and bring her back home. I pray that He will save such a beautiful soul to continue to walk with Him, because nothing is impossible to God the Father.

Luke 15:4-7 says,

> *Suppose one of you has a hundred sheep and loses one of them. Doesn't he leave the ninety-nine in the open country and go after the lost sheep until he finds it? And when he finds it, he joyfully puts it on his shoulders and goes home. Then he calls his friends and neighbors together and says, 'Rejoice with me; I have found my lost sheep.' I tell you that in the same way there will be more rejoicing in heaven over one sinner who repents than over ninety-nine righteous persons who do not need to repent.*

God took advantage of my situation and prepared me for who I am in Christ today.

Three

Transported Via Fire

3

"It was at the end of the year 2020 that the Holy Spirit opened my spiritual eyes and made me understand the dream that I had 22 years earlier, when the angels came to take me to heaven through fire."

TRANSPORTED VIA FIRE

> **"As the angels were taking me, I saw that fire was all around us until I made it to heaven."**

Now to my trips. The very first time I ever went to heaven was after I got baptized in 1998 in Haiti.

I remember that as I slept, I saw in a vision of the night, where God sent angels to come get me. As the angels were taking me, I saw that fire was all around us until I made it to heaven.

What would that revelation mean?

Well, one thing I know for sure is that God would never show you something without giving you the meaning. Otherwise, He wouldn't show you anything at all. Even if He doesn't open your understanding to the meaning of what He shows you right away, there will be a time when He will tell you what it means, if you choose to stay in the Word and follow His commandments.

If you give up on Him, you will probably not even remember if you ever had any dream or revelation from God, unless you repent and get back to the Lord. Then, if He wills, He might still reveal to you the truth behind any dream or revelation you've had in the past.

It took 22 years for me to really understand the revelation from God. As a matter of fact, I even forgot about it, and never really gave a thought until I began to write down all my trips to Heaven. I'm grateful to the Father for graciously reminding me.

It was at the end of the year 2020 that the Holy Spirit opened my spiritual eyes and made me understand the dream that I had 22 years earlier, when the angels came to take me to heaven through fire. He made me understand that it was symbolic of the baptism through the Holy Spirit and fire.

Now, you might say this is not what the Bible teaches about the baptism in the Holy Spirit. Well, you see, when John the Baptist was preaching repentance to the people in Matthew 3:11, he said, *I baptize you with water for repentance. But after me comes one who is more powerful than I, whose sandals I am not worthy to carry. He will baptize you with the Holy Spirit and fire.*

And again, in 1Corinthians 10:2 the Apostle Paul said, *For I do not want you to be ignorant of the fact, brothers and sisters, that our ancestors were all under the cloud and that they all passed through the sea. They were all baptized into Moses in the cloud and in the sea.*

As you can see, the Israelites were symbolically baptized in water by going through the sea as the chosen people of God. They were not able to receive the baptism through the Holy Spirit and fire because Christ had not yet been revealed. The latter baptism was only possible by Christ and through Christ.

Now, you can compare the experience of the Israelites to mine. I received the baptism through the Holy Spirit and fire while going to heaven with the angels through fire just like the Israelites received water baptism while going through the sea.

I hope you will understand this revelation the way the Lord interpreted it to me.

The Israelites were symbolically baptized in water by going through the sea as the chosen people of God.

An Invitation to
Worship Service
in Heaven

4

"When I heard them singing, it wasn't with my physical ears. Instead, my heart heard them singing. Yet, I could hear them so loud, just like I would with my ears."

An Invitation to Worship Service in Heaven

> **"** I was wondering that I could hear a song so loud, yet I didn't see the people's lips moving... **"**

This would seem to me, the second greatest trip I had to Heaven.

To start with, my invitation to the Worship Service in Heaven was very special, and made me love God even more. I saw how God cares for me, and I don't see any reason or anything in me that should make Him show me so much love the way He's been doing it.

This was sometime around the year 2020 during the Covid-19 Pandemic. My mother was very sick, and I was blessed to be the only one out of all my siblings to take good care of her. Then God invited me to the Worship Service in Heaven, and I took her with me there.

When I got to Heaven, I went into a Big Room where I saw many people seated and singing a really beautiful song. I can't really tell which song it was, but what shocked me the most was that I heard them all singing that song together, yet their lips weren't moving.

We usually don't stay mute to sing, otherwise, we would be singing in our heart and no one would realize if we're singing or not. If you aren't singing out loud, no one would know what is going on in your heart.

In Heaven, however, when they are singing, you wouldn't know, because their lips aren't moving. So, you would probably think it's just a bunch of lazy people sitting down and doing nothing.

I was wondering that I could hear a song so loud,

yet I didn't see the people's lips moving. They seemed to be mute, and it was so strange to me. Also, when I heard them singing, it wasn't with my physical ears. Instead, my heart heard them singing. Yet, I could hear them so loud, just like I would with my ears.

God the Father knew what I was thinking. So, He told me the reason why I heard them singing without seeing their lips moving. He said it is because they are not singing with their mouths, but with their hearts in one spirit. He said, all of their hearts were connected together, and in order for me to hear them, He connected my heart to theirs.

I could hear the song they were singing. The worship was amazing, unbelievable, and impossible to understand, if God didn't connect you heart-to-heart with them. What really amazed me was the fact that they could sing in their hearts, and once the song was ended, they all stopped together. It was great to have such an experience with God.

The room was designed much like a stadium, or even some big megachurches with rows of seats from top to bottom. When they were all done singing, they got up on their feet and welcomed us by clapping their hands while walking down the stairs to us.

My mother and I stood in the middle of the room, which was a form of a circle, and all of them gathered around us.

I can't really tell why they did what they did. But in all, I can say it was great to have such an experience with God.

The worship was amazing, unbelievable, and impossible to understand, if God didn't connect you heart-to-heart with them.

Five

Healing on
Resurrection Day

5

> "When I went to see a doctor, they found out it was a herniated disc in my lower back. It used to be very painful when I sat down on the floor to play with my son, or if I stood for too long."

5

Healing on Resurrection Day

I saw Jesus Christ wearing a big Gold
Colored Belt. Then He grabbed me and...

The third time I went to heaven, I remember I had terrible back pain.

When I went to see a doctor, they found out it was a herniated disc in my lower back. It used to be very painful when I sat down on the floor to play with my son, or if I stood for too long.

However, there was this Sunday after church service, I went home and took a nap as usual. Then I saw Christ Jesus come to me. He said to me, "Pierre, Pierre, it's me the Lord Jesus. It's time to go home for it's Resurrection Day."

Suddenly I saw many people going up to heaven, and there is this song that everyone was singing, as we went up. It's found in the Book of Revelation 21:4 - *And God will wipe away every tear from their eyes; there shall be no more death, nor sorrow, nor crying. There shall be no more pain, for the former things have passed away.*

When we got to the part of the song that says, "there shall be no more pain," I saw Jesus Christ wearing a big Gold Colored Belt. Then He grabbed me and placed my lower back in front of His Belt.

It was so painful that I tried to put my right hand between my lower back and His Belt to massage it. The Lord Jesus Christ took my right hand off my back and held me so tight to His Belt as we went up through the clouds.

When we got to Heaven, we were in a big place. I can't tell if it was a room. And the people there were so nice to me.

I was looking to see if my son was saved, then I saw him there sitting about the third or fourth row. As I was trying to go sit next to him in the middle, the people began to make room for me to sit next to him.

I saw the Lord Jesus Christ stand as the Pastor and Shepherd of the Church to welcome His Bride to Heaven. It was such an amazing experience.

When I woke up from that revelation, I didn't feel any more pain at all. I was completely healed from my herniated disc. I was able to do the things I couldn't do. I could even go to the gym and lift weights as I loved to do, with no problem at all.

There was another church service that night, and I remember sharing this testimony. It was amazing!

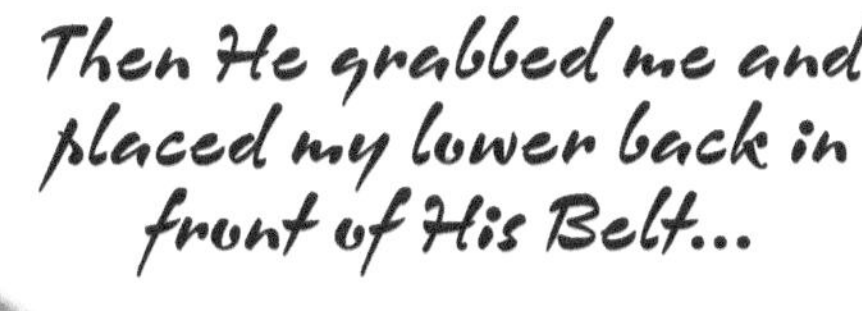

Six

A Great Visit From God the Father

6

"I was looking at Him and said nothing until I woke up in the morning to thank Him for such a visit. He lifted my spirit; I was so happy. I felt great about it, and I was always thanking Him..."

A Great Visit from God the Father

> He said to me, "This is God the Father. I
> saw how your heart needed to see Me, so I..

Have you ever imagined God the Father paying you a visit in your dream?

We have read things like that in the Old Testament and occasionally we can have someone that God appears to, though not often.

Some people have never seen God in their dreams or visions. They merely imagine it. But I have had real experiences, not mere imaginations, as they didn't occur once but many times.

We may say, no one sees God the Father according to Christ Jesus. Yes, no one can ever see God the Father and live, but only the Word of God Who is Christ Jesus Himself. He has seen the Father because He is His Word; He came from Him, and He lives in God the Father as His Word.

In addition, however, many prophets also saw God the Father in their dreams. That's how God communicated with them. God Himself said He would appear in many prophets' dreams to talk to them.

The Great Prophet Isaiah went to Heaven and sat face-to-face with God the Father.

However, you don't have to be a prophet for God to appear to you. And you don't have to think you're a prophet or start claiming that you are higher than others just because God the Father, or His Word, Christ Jesus appeared to you.

Once you start acting that way, God will not continue to use you, because you're already getting far ahead of Him. You need to be very careful when the Lord appears to you.

Never get ahead of someone who is hiring you to work for them. They will either cut you off or never even hire you anymore. We have seen this a lot in the Lord.

There are many that God did call to work for Him, but they wouldn't stay in training, because they don't have the patience to be trained. They think they're ready to work without any training.

If we as humans need anyone starting a job to be trained, how can it be different with God? All the prophets received training from God. He took them away from others for years, so He could train them.

Christ did the same thing with His disciples. He trained them all for years until they were ready to go on their own. Christ always sent them by themselves little by little, until they were completely ready.

But these days we don't really see that, and that's the reason we have more weeds among the wheat.

An Encouraging Visit

One of the most striking revelations I had from God the Father was when I had no place to stay with my son, but to go stay at my office for months with him.

I remember it was ten months after my ex-wife left me. During these ten months, I had a dream, but I never remembered that dream until after it came to reality, then I remembered I already dreamed of it.

I saw in the dream that I was staying at my office and slept in one of the rooms there, even though at that time, I was still at my apartment.

I remember I couldn't afford to pay for both places. I needed to choose to keep just one. So, I decided to put everything in storage and move to the office with my son.

We both slept there for months. People were looking at me weirdly and saying all the bad things about me, especially with my little boy. And they were not wrong, but that was the route God wanted me to take so He could start teaching me.

In His Providence, God permitted me to face real

tough times, so He could make a way for me to start learning the Word at His Feet.

I can say that 100% of the time, God will not start teaching you from a place of comfort. We see this everywhere in the Bible, from the prophets to the Disciples and Apostles of Jesus Christ, and other New Testament believers.

God can allow you to face tough and uncomfortable situations in life. He can allow you to go through tough experiences that would make you question Him. But He will also make sure He is with you during those tough times, so you don't get discouraged.

And because of His constant communication and encouragement, you may not even remember you are in a position of discomfort.

In the beginning, it wasn't easy for me to look at my son sleeping in my office, but when I remembered that I had a dream where I saw myself sleeping at my office months before I moved in there, I knew that God had already shown it to me.

That was where God revealed to me Who Christ

really is, and the difference between Him and Christ. He started to teach me so much about Christ, and I never had to worry about where I was sleeping with my son, because right there I was getting so much from God, all the time.

Jesus appeared to me many times. God spoke to me a few times. And my whole teaching about Christ Jesus started there at the office. That was where I knew Who Christ really is.

Beloved, think for a moment, what really makes your flesh uncomfortable? I can say it's the old man that's still alive in you. If that old man is uncomfortable, you will be uncomfortable, because the old man always wants you to feel good in your body. He always wants you to please yourself.

God's Spirit works the exact opposite. When God's Spirit takes over your spirit and makes it comfortable, you won't have to worry about your flesh being uncomfortable, because your fleshly desires have got nothing to do with God's Spirit.

It's not like it's tough to live for God! It's the old man that makes it hard to live for Him. Once the old man is crucified with Christ, we no longer live for the devil but God alone.

The great Apostle Paul stated in Galatians 2:19-20, *For I through the law died to the law that I might live to God. I have been crucified with Christ; it is no longer I who live, but Christ lives in me; and the life which I now live in the flesh I live by faith in the Son of God, who loved me and gave Himself for me.*

I remember when God told me He wants me to be dead in the flesh; He wants me to be crucified with His Word, Christ, Who is living in me; He wants to stone my fleshly desire to death; He wants to slice me in pieces; He wants to burn me at the Cross.

I did not know how it would feel for real. It's the toughest life to ever live for God, to accept to let Him crucify the old man with Christ. His Word goes deep inside your heart to dig out all your fleshly desires, so you can become the perfect work of God through Christ.

For me, it was the toughest moment ever in my life, with my six-year-old son sleeping at the office with me. Yet, despite our situation, my heart was still seeking after God desperately, and He saw this.

One night, God appeared in my dream. "Pierre," He called to me.

I answered, "Yes."

He said to me, "This is God the Father. I saw how your heart needed to see Me, so I came for you to see Me."

I was looking at Him and said nothing until I woke up in the morning to thank Him for such a visit. He lifted my spirit; I was so happy. I felt great about it, and I was always thanking Him for being with me during my rough days.

I had gone through so much in my life. I had no one to support me but God alone. He took everyone away from me so I could only rely on Him. It felt like I was in the wilderness all alone with my son. But the Lord appeared to me so many times when there was no one else around me.

He filled all my emptiness. He made me get so used to His visits that if I spent a few months without seeing Him, I got really worried. I would start examining myself to know what was wrong.

However, every time I started to get worried from

the deepest part of my heart, God the Father, or His Word, Christ Jesus would show up to me, so I could have relief and continue to count on them. Now, after all He has done in me, I have experienced the most peaceful life I could ever live for Him.

Jesus Christ tells us in Matthew 11:28-30, *Come to Me, all you who labor and are heavy laden, and I will give you rest. Take My yoke upon you and learn from Me, for I am gentle and lowly in heart, and you will find rest for your souls. For My yoke is easy and My burden is light.*

Once you fully come to God the Father through Christ the Word, you will no longer be a slave of sin. You will be able to live a peaceful life, no matter what you're facing, because with God you will gain continual victory, and He will cause you to trample on your enemies.

The Election of Grace:
Another Startling Visit

7

> He put His Hands on my shoulders and said, "I put my Hands on you. I have chosen you. I choose whom I want to choose to work for Me."

THE ELECTION OF GRACE: ANOTHER STARTLING VISIT

> " I knelt before Him... He spoke so softly and kindly to me, "Pierre, this is Me the Lord... "

Paul the Apostle describing Israel talks about *The Election of Grace*. He said in Romans 11:5-6, *Even so then at this present time also there is a remnant according to the election of grace. And if by grace, then is it no more of works: otherwise grace is no more grace.*

Then again, he said in Romans 9:15-16, *For he*

saith to Moses, I will have mercy on whom I will have mercy, and I will have compassion on whom I will have compassion. So then it is not of him that willeth, nor of him that runneth, but of God that sheweth mercy.

Now, you might wonder exactly what I'm trying to make of these Scriptures. In just a short while, you will fully understand.

Well, after my wife left me, I was devastated. A month went by, and I was lonely, miserable, and didn't know what to do. The devil took advantage of my condition and began to whisper a lot of ills to my mind.

He told me to kill myself, that God won't make my wife come back to me. He told me God doesn't love me and is not doing anything for me. He asked me why I would continue to live such a miserable life.

And because of how devastating the situation was for me, I would have actually harmed myself, but God used my son to preserve my life. To tell the truth, my son was the person I was thinking about, if I ever went ahead to do such a thing.

The question of who was going to raise my son literally kept me alive. My son was four years old at that time. He loved me so much and until today, still does.

But then, no one could comfort me in my pains. I remember when a cousin of mine came from Haiti to help me with the pain that I was going through, and right in front of her, I told God that I didn't ever want to serve Him anymore, and that He's been wasting my time, and doesn't care for me.

I told Him that all I want to do is to go serve the devil because the devil takes care of his wicked people, but He (God), as the Most High, can't give me my wife back.

I was so mad at God, and my prayer life suffered as a result. I began to have blood pressure problems and even thought I was going to have a heart attack.

It had become really clear to me that I loved my wife more than I loved the Lord. The Lord Jesus told us in Luke 14:26, *If anyone comes to me and does not hate father and mother, wife and children, brothers and sisters yes, even their own life such a person cannot be my disciple.*

I never thought I loved my wife so much, even

more than the Lord, until things happened the way they did.

And beloved, I would love to give you candid advice, to start thinking about the things you own - money, cars, houses, your loved ones, etc. Do you love them more than the Lord?

Well, you may not really know. But I do hope that the Spirit of the Lord brings everything from your heart to light, so you can be your own judge.

One thing I'm grateful to God for, is that in all these things, He still loved me and understood the immaturity of my actions during those painful moments. He never gave up on me, even though I had a bad attitude towards Him during those stormy days. He still had mercy on me.

Dr. Panam Percy Paul's song, "*He knows, He sees, He feels what you feel; He is the One Who cares for you,*" more than explains the Lord's love for me, and His understanding in my situation.

You see, we often think that God just stands aloof to watch us suffer, while He waits to punish our every mistake. But it's not true. Many times, He understands our pain even more than we do. He always has plans in place to make life whole again.

Jeremiah 29:11-12 (TLB) says, *For I know the plans I have for you," says the Lord. "They are plans for good and not for evil, to give you a future and a hope.*

Even though the devil attacked my mind in every way he could, and tried to take over my spirit to make me become one of his own, my God would never let that happen! He had long chosen me, even before I was born.

Let's consider the great Apostle John's vision on the Island of Patmos. In Revelation 1:17, when the Apostle John saw Christ in his vision, he said, *When I saw him, I fell at his feet as if I were dead. But he laid his right hand on me and said, 'Don't be afraid! I am the First and the Last.'*

That was exactly what happened to me when I saw Christ appear at my house in a vision. Before I reveal what He said to me, let me first say what I noticed: the Power that's in Jesus Christ makes all flesh bow down.

No matter how rich you are; no matter your titles on earth; no matter who you are, trust me, just like the Apostle Paul tells us in Philippians 2:10-

11, *that at the name of Jesus every knee should bow, in heaven and on earth and under the earth, and every tongue confess that Jesus Christ is Lord, to the glory of God the Father.*

We also find this in the Book of Isaiah 45:22-23, when God said, *I have sworn by Myself; The word has gone out of My mouth in righteousness, And shall not return, That to Me every knee shall bow, Every tongue shall take an oath.*

In these two verses, you clearly see that Jesus Christ is God, because no one will bow before God and before Christ at the same time. It's only One Person that every knee shall bow, and every tongue shall confess to, and that person is Jesus Christ.

The reason why I took these two passages as examples is that I don't see how someone will see Christ and not bow before Him as if he were dead. You will not notice it, but the power in Him will make you bow down as if you were dead, as the great Apostle John and myself had experienced. And I am sure many other people have experienced that as well.

Now, there was this precious morning when I

woke up and walked into my living room. Then, I heard God speak within my heart. I could hear His Voice deep in my heart saying to me, "Go back to bed." I didn't resist His Smooth Gentle Voice but simply obeyed.

I went immediately to bed, and just about ten seconds after, I saw a Man in a vision stand in the middle of my room. I knelt before Him just like the Apostle John did when Christ appeared to him on the Island of Patmos. He spoke so softly and kindly to me, *"Pierre, this is Me the Lord Christ."*

He put His Hands on my shoulders and said, *"I put my Hands on you. I have chosen you. I choose whom I want to choose to work for Me."*

Right then, I noticed hot tears flowing out of my eyes as I cried to Him, "Why choose me? Why me among all of the people who are serving You?"

I was not able to see His entire Body, but just His upper body from His face to His chest and His Feet. And His Feet were just as described in Revelation 1:15 (NLT) – *His feet were like polished bronze refined in a furnace,...*

Once He left me, I opened my eyes and said to

myself, "What just happened to me? I went to lie down on the bed, and within seconds all of that happened to me?"

I can tell that this is what's called being in eternity, because there is no such thing as time there. God can show you or teach you in a vision so much in a split of seconds.

I immediately went on my knees and began to thank God for such a Divine visit. And with a contrite and open heart, I asked the Lord to forgive me for all the wrong utterances I made in my pain. The Lord opened His Arms to receive me and forgave all my sins.

Since then, the Lord never stopped talking to me, taking me to heaven, and teaching me His Word. This wasn't because I was that good, flawless man, but rather because He had chosen me according to the election of grace.

Whenever I spoke to people about what the Lord was doing in my life, they thought I was crazy. They would look at me like, "Who are you for God to appear to you?" What they failed to understand is that it wasn't about who I was but what God had planned and chosen to do through me.

Remember beloved, that the Bible says, *It is he who saved us and chose us for his holy work not because we deserved it but because that was his plan long before the world began-to show his love and kindness to us through Christ* (2Timothy 1:9, TLB).

God will do what He will do with your life, not exactly because you deserve it, but because it was His plan long before you were born. This, I believe, should act as a solid base for your understanding of my many experiences with the Lord.

One-on-One With God

A few months after, God pulled me out of the church I used to attend and made me stay home in confinement to serve Him, so He could teach me His ways and His Word one-on-one.

When I shared this with a few Christians, they really thought I had a demon. Some even thought I left the church because I wanted to go back to the world. They never understood, but I had to do what the Lord told me to do.

That the Lord pulled me out does not mean something was wrong with the church. Rather, whenever God calls someone as a chosen one to teach them, He never leaves them in the crowds. He always takes them away from everyone else.

He mostly takes them to the wilderness for whatever He wants to teach them, as can be seen with all the prophets He called. He took them far away from the crowds.

Even Christ never taught His disciples among the crowd. He always took them away to go teach them the Word of God. And I'm sure that's one of the reasons He took me out of the local church.

You think it was easy for me to leave the local church? Absolutely not, because I had no one else to rely on or talk to. And most especially, with the tradition of men, that if you don't go to church, you're going to hell, it wasn't an easy decision.

To avoid being misunderstood, I'm not saying that you shouldn't go to church. Of course, you must go to church. The church is the best place to be. Even though we see or hear all manner of things happening among us, the true church of God remains perfect inside the local church.

Try to be a perfect church inside the local church. I'm not talking about the local church being perfect, not at all. If you ever believe any of the local churches is perfect, then you're misleading yourself and you're still in the dark.

The Lord Jesus Christ tells us in Matthew 13:25, *But while everyone was sleeping, his enemy came and sowed weeds among the wheat, and went away. The devil spreads his weeds all over the church. That's why many churches appear to be upside down. But Jesus has control of His people that are among the weeds in the local churches.*

Just be very careful with all the false pastors, false prophets, and fake leaders who only ask you to bring them money and God will bless you. These are false leaders, weeds who are among the wheat. Run away from such places and ask God to guide you somewhere else.

Nevertheless, as I've already stated, you must always attend your local church unless God clearly speaks to you that He wants to have a one-on-one with you. Still, you have to make sure it's really God that tells you that. The devil can always speak to deceive you. But you will know when it's God telling you to do so, because you will see the work that He has started in you.

God will make sure that you know it's Him. I'm sure He may appear to you to tell you what exactly He wants to do with you. Other than that, you must go to church. If not, you will be tempted and fall into sin.

I can tell you that up till today, God keeps me pure. No woman can accuse me of having an affair with them. That's what God can do with you, if you really want to serve Him. There are no excuses to think that you can't live for God without having an affair with someone.

> *Many times, He understands our pain even more than we do...*

Eight

God's Test

8

"After He handed me the test on a sheet of paper, I saw many questions, yet I couldn't even read the first question. It's like I was Haitian, yet given a test in Chinese - impossible."

GOD'S TEST

Days after the Lord Jesus Christ appeared to me at my house and put His Hands on me as His chosen, I had a "test" encounter. And, I think that anyone the Lord calls to do His work has to go through some test.

Also, I think that no one can ever answer any of

God's questions in the flesh, not to talk of pass His test.

The very first person who failed God's test was Adam. Yet, he was the only person in the Old Testament who had all of the chances not to fail, because he was the firstborn of God among mankind.

Adam didn't come from mankind. He was created by the Hands of God the Father, and was living in a perfect body. He wasn't conceived or born in sins like we are. Yet, he failed God's test! And after he failed, everyone else inherited his sins until today.

As you can imagine, if Adam who wasn't born in sins, but instead was created by God the Father failed, who else in the entire world wouldn't fail?

There was no way Adam wasn't going to fail God's test, except God the Father never cast down the devil and all his wicked angels.

Once He cast them down, the earth was going to be some difficult terrain for Adam and Eve, and the rest of mankind who came from them.

God knew that mankind would never be able to follow His Word unless the Word was living in them. At that time, the Word of God Who is Jesus Christ the Messiah wasn't living in Adam and Eve. If the Word of God was living in them, they wouldn't sin.

The time had not yet come for the Word of God to live in mankind until the Word of God was made flesh, and dwelled among men.

In the Garden of Eden, the Word of God was only given to them as instructions to follow. God instructed them not to eat the fruit from the tree of knowledge of good and evil. And when they sinned, He thrust them out of the Garden, so they wouldn't eat of the Tree of Life.

Many people are still wondering what the Tree of Life represents in the Bible. That question has been answered in the sequel to this book, which is loaded with revelations.

Why did I say the Word of God, which is Christ, was not made flesh yet to live in mankind? It's because I want to show the difference between 'when the Word of God is given to you,' and 'when the Word of God is living in you.'

When God spoke to Adam and Eve, He gave them instructions on what to do or what not to do. They had the choice either to follow God's instructions or not. And they chose not to follow His instructions. That's why they both sinned.

If Adam and Eve Had the Word of God (Christ Jesus) living in them like the Apostles and Christians of today, they wouldn't sin, because the perfect Word of God (Christ Jesus) would be living in their perfect body.

I know someone would be thinking, "Hey! But today's Christians sin!" Of course, yes. Today's Christians aren't living in a perfect body like Adam and Eve were. We all live in sinful flesh.

That's why the Apostle Paul said, *I don't really understand myself, for I want to do what is right, but I don't do it. Instead, I do what I hate. So I am not the one doing wrong; it is sin living in me that does it* **Romans 7:15,17** (NLT).

But you see, Adam and Eve weren't living in this sinful body that the Apostle Paul describes. They were living in perfect bodies. So, the point here is that if Adam and Eve, while living in their perfect bodies, also had the Word of God (Christ Jesus) living in them, they wouldn't sin.

And come to think of it, in the ongoing battle against our sinful flesh, we would have been worse, if it weren't for Christ, the Word of God Who is living in us.

The reason why I say we would have been worse isn't because we are not serving the Lord but because we, as Christians, could do better in the Lord by obeying the Holy Spirit.

We must take advantage of the sacrifice that Christ Jesus made for us, to walk by the Holy Spirit just like the Church did at the beginning.

I would believe that Adam and Eve, the prophets, and everyone else in the Old Testament wished to have the privilege of the Word of God living in them as we have today.

Imagine that you are living in a perfect body like Adam and Eve were in the beginning, and, in addition, have Christ as the Word of God living in you! That would be powerful, right!

Well, we as true Christians will one day live in a perfect body just like Adam and Eve were, and have Christ Jesus living in us forever. Our hearts will follow the Word of God (Christ Jesus) everywhere He goes, and we will never sin again.

So, you see what Adam and Eve were missing while living in the perfect body: The Word of God (Jesus Christ) living in them.

Now, if mankind continued to live like Adam and Eve in the fallen state, the end would have been the lake of fire. *But God so loved the world that He gave His One and only Son* (The Word of God), *that whosoever believes in Him* (The Word of God) *shall not perish but have eternal life* (**John 3:16**, Emphasis mine).

The Word of God (The Son) was made Flesh, and died for our sins so we could be One with His Word (That is, Himself). And once we are made One with Him (His Word), it's a totally different thing.

When we are one with the Word, God is not only speaking His Word, which is Christ Jesus to mankind, but He has His Word living in those who accept Him and become His children.

Adam and Eve were not the only ones who failed God's test, but everyone else who came after them - Noah, Moses, Abraham, Enoch, all the prophets, and everyone else that God called to do His work.

We also see Job who was tremendously being tested by God, and he couldn't answer even one of God's questions.

Why?

Because no one can ever pass God's test except in one condition, and the only one: "Christ Jesus living in you." And He will be the only One to pass the test in you.

From Adam and Eve to the prophets, and until Christ started preaching repentance, no one could ever pass God's test. God just used them all to do His work, but many of them were not doing His will heartily, because the old man was still living in them, and wasn't crucified yet.

Listen! There is no way you can do God's will with the old man living in you.

That same old man who was living in Adam and Eve and all the people in the Old Testament, was crucified with Christ on the cross so that the body of sin would no longer dominate us, and we would no longer be enslaved to sin.

Romans 6:6 says, *Knowing this, that our old man is crucified with him, that the body of sin might be destroyed, that henceforth we should not serve sin.*

Take a look at the life of Jesus' disciples after Jesus Christ was raised from the dead. You truly can tell after Christ got resurrected from the dead, that all the disciples were doing God's work with no complaints at all, but with joy and happiness.

They were all ready to die for the work of God. They gave their lives completely as a burned sacrifice offered to God.

They saw death, and rather than run away from it, they ran towards it. We have read of how most of the disciples were killed. Some were stoned to death, and others burned alive in churches.

Some were nailed on the cross, and others were thrown into boiling oil. Some were dragged along the bare ground and others were beheaded because of their testimony about Jesus and because of the Word of God.

The disciples went through the worst of torture, yet they never gave up and never got discouraged. Instead, they were encouraging each other to die for God's work; something that none of the prophets were willing to do.

The disciples were never hiding like the prophets who were afraid of death back then. It wasn't the fault of those prophets, but the old man who was living in them instead of Jesus Christ. They were neither made One with the Word of God (Christ Jesus) nor guided by the Holy Spirit.

Now you can see the difference between the people in the Old Testament and the people in the New Testament. They were both given a test to take so they could be chosen by God to continue to work for Him with no complaints, hesitation, and hate.

So, which of the two groups most likely passed the test?

Well, we all know that none of the two groups could pass the test, but since the old man got crucified as a burnt sacrifice, he is completely dead in those who are in Christ and should no longer be living in them. Christ Jesus is the One living in us after the old man who lived in us got crucified with Christ on the cross.

So, Christ is the One answering all the questions for us. He is the One Who is taking the test for us and passing it. That's why we shouldn't boast about anything that's done in us by God.

My Moment of Test

I remember when God put me in Heaven to sit down on a chair by myself in a room. He appeared to me as an Older person with a long white robe.

After He handed me the test on a sheet of paper, I saw many questions, yet I couldn't even read the first question. It's like I was Haitian, yet given a test in Chinese - impossible.

I was like, if I can't even read the first question, how then am I supposed to be able to read and answer the rest of the questions? I was unhappy because I was unable to read and answer the questions.

Furthermore, God only showed me His Back. And because I only saw His back, I didn't know if it was God or not.

Then I called to Him, and He turned around. But I still didn't know if it was Him. So, I raised my voice and said, "Why would you give me a test when I can't even read the first question? How am

I supposed to pass it?"

He looked at me and allowed me to know it's Him talking to me. Immediately, fear gripped me. With an angry Voice, He said, "Pierre, sit down where I put you to sit down, and you will not get up from that chair until you pass the test."

Well, that happened to be the same year my ex-wife left me; just about two to three months after, to be exact. I thought I was ready to pass the test, but I was complaining about not having my wife come back to me, and about everything else that was going on in my life.

The Lord saw I wasn't being patient. I was like a fool that knew nothing about what God wanted to do in me. The only thing that was of interest to me was my wife's return. That was all my flesh wanted.

God let me take the test once, so I could see that I wasn't ready. I stood in a long line where many people came to take the test. As I got in front of God, I couldn't even answer the first question from Him.

Then God started to teach me patience, and I remember the Spirit of God always telling me to ask God for a lot of patience, wisdom, and all the fruit of the Spirit of God. I kept on reading the Bible and kept writing the Hidden Truth About Jesus Christ.

Passing God's Test

In the year 2020, God Himself brought me to that room in Heaven to take the test, again. This time, it wasn't me rushing Him. I gave up after I had failed the first test. I was concentrating to let the work of God be done in me.

After I finished the whole test, God said to me, "You passed the test 200/200." I was so happy that I finally made it.

But He said to me, "You didn't pass the test by yourself, but Christ Who is living in you passed it for you."

Once I heard that, I got even happier. Then God made me realize that no one can ever pass His examination from their flesh with that old man not being crucified in them.

So, everyone in the Old Testament from Adam to the prophets, and until Christ started to preach repentance, failed God's exam. If we could ever do God's work without Christ living in our lives, then "Christ died in vain."

Understanding God's Test

I know some people might be wondering what test I wrote in Heaven and had such high scores.

Well, the test that was given to me was not literal. Rather, it was about my calling to God Who chose me for His work. Thus, He had a lot of work to do in me first - to train me, prepare me, teach me, and build me up. And it all had to be done in Christ.

All through Scriptures, we see God's preparation of the prophets, the Apostles, and everyone He chooses to use, including our brothers and sisters all around us.

God will always prepare you first for what He intends to do with your life, because the army that He is preparing you to go against, isn't ordinary. It has to do with satan and his host of demons, the most powerful wicked army in the universe.

The Apostle Paul says in 2Corinthians 10:3-6,

For though we live in the world, we do not wage war as the world does. The weapons we fight with are not the weapons of the world. On the contrary, they have divine power to demolish strongholds. We demolish arguments and every pretension that sets itself up against the knowledge of God, and we take captive every thought to make it obedient to Christ. And we will be ready to punish every act of disobedience, once your obedience is complete.

Only God's Army can destroy the devil's host of wickedness in a split of seconds. But you must be well trained to be a part of God's Army. And that can only be done by the Most Powerful trainer, the Most Powerful Commander-in-Chief, and the Most Powerful General, Who is Jesus Christ alone.

That is why the Apostle Paul said in Colossians 1:16-17, *For in him all things were created: things in heaven and on earth, visible and invisible, whether thrones or powers or rulers or authorities; all things have been created through him and for him. He is before all things, and in him all things hold together.*

If Christ has control of everything that was created in Heaven and on earth, visible and invisible, whether thrones or powers or rulers or authorities, why wouldn't you as God's soldier, want to be in Christ Jesus, so you can be a part of the Most Powerful and Most Protected Army?

You have to be a part of God's Army, otherwise, you will lose against satan and his demons.

Remember, while being trained, you will be going through fires, waters, rivers, storms, and all kinds of hardships that are meant to toughen and fully prepare you for spiritual warfare.

And, God Who is your Trainer, your General, and Commander-in-Chief, will always be with you to strengthen you, help you, and uphold you with His righteous Right Hand as He promised.

1Peter 1:6-7 says,

> *In this you greatly rejoice, though now for a little while, if need be, you have been grieved by various trials, so that the proven character of your faith—more precious than gold, which perishes even though refined by fire—may result in praise, glory, and honor at the revelation of Jesus Christ....*

Nine

The Reality of God's Voice

THE VOICE OF GOD

9

> "He would always say, "Remember my promise to you. Remember it wasn't someone that came and told you about Me, or gave you a message from Me. I spoke to you directly, and it was loud and clear.""

9

THE REALITY OF GOD'S VOICE

> " I remember that evening when I heard His Voice. I would never forget that moment. "

To hear God's Voice is something special to me. It means everything. The day I heard God's voice, I was strengthened. And to be able to hear His Voice also gives me a good reason not to stab Him from His back while He was always with me during all my tough times.

We see in the Bible how God communicated with His prophets, His chosen ones, and others. Ask yourself a simple question: Does God still speak to people these days? Of course, yes! But it depends on your relationship with Him through His Word.

I heard His voice loud and clear when He spoke to me. I've heard and seen the Word speak with me. I understand that I can hear His voice, but when I say, I've seen His Word speaking to me, what do I really mean?

Yes, I've seen God's Word many times. Whenever I say I've seen Jesus Christ talking to me, it's not just Jesus as a Person talking to me like most people think; it's actually God the Father talking to me through His Word, Jesus Christ.

You see, Jesus Christ is not a Person with a different mindset than God talking to you. It is no one else but God the Father alone talking to you.

Like I said above, God the Father just allowed the Apostles, the Disciples, and many of us to be able to see His perfect Word, Who is Jesus Christ.

This is the same Person that the people in the Old Testament wished to see face-to-face, or even saw in their dreams.

I remember that evening when I heard His voice. I would never forget that moment. Every time I get discouraged, feel like giving up in hard times, don't see what to do or where to go, God always brings that day to my attention.

He would always say, "Remember my promise to you. Remember it wasn't someone that came and told you about Me, or gave you a message from Me. I spoke to you directly, and it was loud and clear."

There is no way you can remember that and choose to give up!

Even though I've seen God the Father and the Lord Jesus Christ many times, in my journeys to Heaven, to be able to hear God's Voice while awake isn't something I can ignore. That's the one thing that still makes me keep on going with the Lord, no matter how crazy life is for me.

While I lay on my couch, I heard someone call my name. I was shocked, and I answered, "Yes!"

The Voice said, "This is God the Father. I see what you've been going through. I will not leave you or forsake you, for I will always be with you."

Only God really knew what I was going through. And, I believe, for me not to harm myself, because of the great mission He had for me, He would sometimes come and talk to me, and take me to Heaven.

It's not because I did anything special, but instead, He made me special in His eyes. As you know, there is not one person that can do anything special to make God satisfied. Only when He chooses you to work for Him, then He will be satisfied in the work that He has done in you through Christ.

God is real!

God is great!

God is faithful!

It is my hope, that you will never give up on the Lord our God.

I always pray to God to make others experience what I've been experiencing with Him, so that more people can believe in Him. I pray that they can experience Him and accept His Word in their lives. And that they will accept to live by that Word, and die in that Word.

Jesus Christ is that Precious and perfect Word of God Who is One with God forever, just like your word is one with you. The only difference is, God's Word was made flesh for mankind to see that mystery.

John 1:14 says, *And the Word was made flesh, and dwelt among us, (and we beheld his glory, the glory as of the only begotten of the Father,) full of grace and truth.*

He is before all things. He is that Word God spoke for the first time when He created the universe from the beginning (Colossians 1:15; Proverbs 8:22 - more details on these Scriptures in the next volume).

It is a great blessing to hear God speaking to me. It is a great delight to experience the reality of His Voice.

Learning at the Feet
of God the Father

10

"
While that was on, God called me up
to Heaven. This time around, no
angels came to get me. Jesus Christ
didn't come to get me as well.
I went by myself as a grown
child in the Lord.
"

LEARNING AT THE FEET OF GOD THE FATHER

> **"** I looked down to see where I was putting my feet. When I looked down, I saw I was walking on the clouds... **"**

Sitting with God the Father face-to-face in Heaven wasn't something that I expected from Him. So, for some reason, I feel like I'm one of the most blessed persons on earth.

I'm not the only person who is blessed with this experience. Many prophets in Scripture also saw

God either in their visions or dreams. For example, Moses in the Book of Exodus 33:17-22,

> *And the LORD said to Moses, "I will do the very thing you have asked, because I am pleased with you and I know you by name."*
>
> *Then Moses said, "Now show me your glory."*
>
> *And the LORD said, "I will cause all my goodness to pass in front of you, and I will proclaim my name, the LORD, in your presence. I will have mercy on whom I will have mercy, and I will have compassion on whom I will have compassion.*
>
> *But," he said, "you cannot see my face, for no one may see me and live."*
>
> *Then the LORD said, "There is a place near me where you may stand on a rock.*
>
> *When my glory passes by, I will put you in a cleft in the rock and cover you with my hand until I have passed by.*
>
> *Then I will remove my hand and you will see my back; but my face must not be seen.*

Just imagine that you see God's glory passing in

front of you. How would you feel?

I don't think there will ever be a prophet like Moses ever on earth.

I have personally heard God's voice loud and clear only once, but Moses was talking to God all the time, especially when He went for 40 days and nights with God the Father on Mount Sinai.

Moses didn't just end there. He was in communication with the Father all the time.

There are many other prophets that saw God in their dreams. God Himself mentioned that in the Book of Numbers 12:6-7,

> *Listen to my words: "When there is a prophet among you, I, the LORD, reveal myself to them in visions, I speak to them in dreams. But this is not so with My servant Moses; he is faithful in all My house...."*

Also, in Genesis 32:30 Jacob said, *for I have seen God face to face, and my life is preserved.*

Furthermore, Isaiah 6:1 shows how the Prophet Isaiah saw God.

> *In the year that King Uzziah died, I saw the*

Lord, high and exalted, seated on a throne; and the train of his robe filled the temple.

Above him were seraphim, each with six wings: With two wings they covered their faces, with two they covered their feet, and with two they were flying.

And they were calling to one another: "Holy, holy, holy is the LORD Almighty, the whole earth is full of his glory."

At the sound of their voices the doorposts and thresholds shook, and the temple was filled with smoke.

"Woe to me!" I cried. "I am ruined! For I am a man of unclean lips, and I live among a people of unclean lips, and my eyes have seen the King, the LORD Almighty."

Then one of the seraphim flew to me with a live coal in his hand, which he had taken with tongs from the altar.

With it he touched my mouth and said, "See, this has touched your lips; your guilt is taken away and your sin atoned for."

The same way God made His chosen people see Him is the same way He is still doing it these days. The same God yesterday is the same today and forever.

The Apostle Paul said in 2Corinthians 12:2, *I know a man in Christ who fourteen years ago was caught up to the third heaven. Whether it was in the body or out of the body I do not know~God knows.*

I am sure that the Apostle Paul saw God or the Word of God, even though he didn't mention it.

I've reiterated some verses in the Bible so it's clear that there were other people that God also chose to appear to and talk to as well.

Face-to-Face With God

I was in a dream preaching to people that the church will be raptured before the great tribulation. Right among the people, there was a man listening to me, who had a great relationship with the Lord, and knew God's Word.

He said, Lord! "I heard brother Pierre preaching that Jesus Christ is coming before the great tribulation. Is that true?"

The Lord said to him, "Don't worry; I'll take care of Pierre."

While that was on, God called me up to Heaven. This time around, no angels came to get me. Jesus Christ didn't come to get me as well. I went by myself as a grown child in the Lord.

As I got up there, I went straight in front of the Lord Jesus Christ. I saw Him sit on His Throne when I got there. And He got up to greet me. Then He said, "Let Me go show you My Father."

As I walked on His left side, I looked down to see where I was putting my feet. When I looked down, I saw I was walking on the clouds. They were beautiful.

When I got in front of God the Father, I saw Him sit on His Throne facing South, and there was a chair reserved for me to sit down. Incidentally, the Lord Jesus disappeared, and it was me and the Father sitting face-to-face.

As I sat down, I looked to my left and saw many angels coming from underneath with something in their hands. I couldn't tell what they were holding in their hands, as I was not able to see their faces at all. They were all in white clothing, and I could only see their eyes but their faces were covered.

God the Father knew that my heart needed to know who those were in His omniscience. So, He said to the angels, "Uncover your face, so My servant can see you." Then all the angels did what God the Father said.

They looked like Humans.

Nevertheless, my focus wasn't on the angels because God the Father was my priority at that time.

I turned my head to face God the Father as He was teaching me concerning the resurrection of the Saints which would take place during the Pre-Tribulation, Mid-Tribulation, and Post-Tribulation.

He was also teaching me The Hidden Truth About Who Jesus Christ really is.

I know that this is a subject that many people are always asking:

"When is Jesus Christ coming back? Will it be Pre-Tribulation, Mid-Tribulation, or

Post–Tribulation that Christ will come?"

I have explained this well in the sequel to this book.

This trip was the most stunning among all the eight trips I made to Heaven.

Just to be able to go to Heaven is special, but to be able to sit down face-to-face in Heaven with God the Father just like the Prophet Isaiah did, was exhilarating, to say the least.

The only difference between me and the Prophet Isaiah is that, since I was in Christ, all my sins were already forgiven, and I was purified by the Word of God.

Isaiah the prophet didn't have Christ back then. That was the reason his sins were apparent, but God made provision for his sins to be forgiven when he got to Heaven as you already read in Isaiah 6:5-7.

You might be asking, "But Brother Pierre, how did you see Heaven? What did you see? Is it beautiful?"

Well, I can't really tell you much about the beauty

of Heaven because God the Father didn't really allow me to see too many things up there. Maybe in another trip, He will if it's His will.

The beauty of Heaven was not why God called me to Heaven, but rather so He could teach me the things He wanted me to know, which is the truth about His Word.

> To be able to sit face-to-face in Heaven with God the Father was exhilarating, to say the least.

Eleven

"Anything You Need,
Just Ask Me."

ASK ME anything

"He stood next to me where His shoulder met mine, so close that not even a tint of smoke could go in between. Our shoulders were as close as the L-corner of a wall."

"ANYTHING YOU NEED, JUST ASK ME."

> Then He added, "Whatever you need to know about Me, just ask Me,..."

God has been teaching me so much about His Word Jesus Christ. In this chapter, I share how the Lord appeared to me and said I should ask Him anything in His Word, which is Christ, if it is in His will, and also isn't to satisfy my flesh or to show off.

Prior to this, I always prayed regularly, asking

God for wisdom as James 1:5 tells us:

> *If any of you lacks wisdom, he should ask God, who gives generously to all without finding fault, and it will be given to him.*

You know, if you are truly seeking the Lord, you can't leave His promises behind. God challenges us to ask Him the things He promised us in His Word, because He will never go against His Word. And, if you're really seeking God heartily, He will give you what you ask for in His will.

While I was sleeping, I saw the Lord Jesus Christ come into my bedroom. Then He said to me, "Pierre, this is the Lord Jesus Christ."

Then, He stood next to me where His shoulder met mine, so close that not even a tint of smoke could go in between. Our shoulders were as close as the L-corner of a wall.

He said to me, "Do you see how tightly close My Shoulder is to yours?"

I said, "Yes!"

He said to me, "It's the same way I'm close to you, and nothing can get in between. Nothing can separate us."

Then He added, "Whatever you need to know about Me, just ask Me, and I will tell you."

I was staring at Him like a woman who is getting married to her lovely man, standing in front of him, holding hands together, staring at him and can't even take her eyes off him, waiting for everything to be over, so she can go for honeymoon with her husband.

That's the way I was taking my time staring at the Lord Jesus Christ the whole time that He was with me, and couldn't wait to enjoy the Lord more in my heart, to feel Him deeply living in me, to be made One with me, and to live with Him forever.

I also realized something in the Lord's Eyes. When He looked at me, He allowed me to see in His eyes Who He really is, which is Love, Forgiveness, Compassion, Humility, Wisdom, and more.

There is no word to describe Him when He allows you to know Who He is. I will always be grateful to the Lord for sharing and showing all of these to me.

Twelve

When Christ Showed Me His Distance

12

"But I was so used to His presence already. I felt that He wasn't carrying me any longer, just like a child that really got used to his parents for years, and wouldn't want to be left alone."

When Christ Showed Me His Distance

> **God sometimes steps back from those who say they love Him but are backstabbing...**

There are times when you feel abandoned by God, but is it really true you're abandoned? No! God says He will never leave us nor forsake us, unless you're not His child. A great Father would never do such a thing.

I'm sure many other people feel the same way I felt. I always hear people say that God gave up on them, especially when things aren't going their way. Well, it's okay to feel that way; even Jesus Christ felt the same way when He was on the Cross.

Many others in the Bible had felt that way, too. The disciples of Jesus also felt that way when Christ was crucified. They didn't see Him for a while, and all of them went back fishing.

There are so many other occasions when people always feel like God has forgotten about them.

Listen! God sometimes steps back from those who say they love Him but are backstabbing Him, and repeating the same mistakes over and over. They think they can play God, or be smart with Him whenever they want to. But God will definitely stay away from such.

The great Apostle Paul tells us in 2Corinthians 6:14-18,

> *Do not team up with those who are unbelievers. How can righteousness be a partner with wickedness? How can light live with darkness? What harmony can there be between Christ and the devil? How can a believer be a partner with an unbeliever? And what union can there*

be between God's temple and idols? For we are the temple of the living God. As God said: "I will live in them and walk among them. I will be their God, and they will be my people. Therefore, come out from among unbelievers, and separate yourselves from them, says the LORD. Don't touch their filthy things, and I will welcome you. And I will be your Father, and you will be my sons and daughters, says the LORD Almighty.

This is a great example from the Apostle Paul. How can you feel God's presence in your life when you're living that kind of life?

How can God use you as His Temple like He used Jesus Christ, the disciples, and many other faithful believers?

God doesn't use just anyone, but those who keep His Temple clean.

I love the 16th verse:

And what union can there be between God's temple and idols? For we are the temple of the living God. As God said: "I will live in them and walk among them. I will be their God, and they will be my people.

I know some people might say, who can be like Christ? Or, who can be perfect like Christ was?

Well, I can tell you that God's goal is for us to be like Christ. That's why He sent Christ to come live the perfect life, so we could follow Him and be able to live the same perfect life that He was living on this earth.

Why did Christ live a perfect life on earth? Because He is the perfect Word of the Almighty God. The Word of God was living in God, and was made One with God. That's why Christ was perfect.

Of course, anyone that's made One with God must be as perfect as God, and Christ is the only one that could be made One with God the Father.

Jesus said it! He is the only One that came from the Father, because He is the Word of the Father. So, for us to be like Christ, we must be made One with the Word.

What that means is, the same way Christ was made One with the Father to be perfect, we too must be made One with Christ to inherit God's perfection through Christ. That's the only way we can become as perfect as Christ was while He lived on this earth.

The truth is, mankind will never be One with God the Father if it's not through His Word, Christ Jesus. He said in the fourteenth chapter of John's Gospel, that no one can go to the Father but through Him only.

Jesus Christ is the only way to be One with the Father. And, as long as you're made One with Christ, you're also made One with the Father, because the Word of God and God are One.

If you're in the Word of God which is Christ, then you're automatically made One with both of them.

So, for me to feel like I was totally disconnected from God, it wasn't because I was doing anything wrong, but Christ wanted me to start walking on my own in Him.

There was a time He was holding my hands and carrying me because I was going through so much. He made sure that I could start walking on my own before He let go of my hands.

But I was so used to His presence already. I felt that He wasn't carrying me any longer, just like a child that really got used to his parents for years, and wouldn't want to be left alone.

My son is ten. And he is so used to me that I don't know how I'm going to let go of his hands, so he can be independent of himself.

It was in a vision of the night that the Lord Jesus Christ showed me that I'm not alone. As I bowed down beside my bed to pray, I saw Him stand all the way at the end of the earth. He showed me His distance and said to me,

"This is exactly how you feel the lack of My Presence in your life. Even though you see me that far away from you, I made you feel that way. I showed you the distance that you're feeling for months between us in a physical way, so you could understand it better. But I did it because I wanted to show you how you really feel I'm disconnected from you. In reality, I will never be disconnected from you. I am always near you. I'm ready to catch you if you're ever going to fall. So, don't worry. I'm always with you, even if you don't feel my presence in your life."

After I heard that while looking at Him, I was so happy. And every time I feel that way again, and remember what He told me - no matter what I'm going through - I always count on what He said to me when He distanced Himself from me.

> *It was in a vision of the night that the Lord Jesus Christ showed me that I was not alone.*

Thirteen

Stay Where You Are!

13

"I was ready for an answer from Him on what direction to take. That same night, He came and said to me not to go to any other religion but to stay a Christian."

STAY WHERE YOU ARE!

> **I went and prayed to God that night from my heart. I said to Him, "You know that I...**

There was a time when I was so confused about where to belong. Though I was a church member, I know for sure I didn't have any heavenly relationship with God the Father through Christ the Word.

Perhaps, it's because I wasn't reading the Bible enough for God the Father to reveal Himself to me through the Word. All I knew was to go to church to worship and listen to a sermon, then go home.

People from different denominations often talked to me to join them, but I was always a little confused until God came to my rescue.

Now, the Bible never teaches us religion, but rather to do God's will through Christ Jesus. If you are not being obedient to Jesus Christ as the Only Word of God, just as you should obey God the Father, then you really need to think about who you want to obey, because it's impossible to obey God the Father but not Christ His Word.

John 5:23 says, That all may honor the Son just as they honor the Father. Whoever does not honor the Son does not honor the Father, who sent him.

This verse talks about honoring God's Word (Jesus Christ) first before you think about honoring God. That's because it's through the Word of God (Jesus Christ) that you find all the information about Who God the Father really is.

It is when you empty yourself and come to the Word of God (Jesus Christ) that you receive eternal life from God.

The great Apostle Paul wrote in the Book of Philippians 2:10-11, *at the name of Jesus every knee should bow, of those in heaven, and of those on earth, and of those under the earth, 11 and that every tongue should confess that Jesus Christ is Lord, to the glory of God the Father.*

So, if every knee should bow at the Name of Jesus Christ, it means Christ is receiving glory from everyone; everyone is worshiping Him; everyone is giving Him full respect for Who He is, which is God's Word, equal with God (which means nothing less than God).

And God would never be jealous of His own Word taking His glory, because God and His Word are One. They were never two separate Persons and they shall never be. So, when the Apostle Paul said 'every knee should bow,' He knew what He was talking about.

This Scripture makes it clear that we should serve God by obeying His Word, which is Christ Jesus. If you serve God, you also serve Christ at the same time because you can't obey God without obeying His Word (Christ).

Once you obey God's Word, you are obeying Christ. The Word that God speaks is Christ Jesus. The Word that comes out of His mouth to pass His judgment to all flesh, to commend people, to make any decision, is Jesus Christ.

So, the Word that was spoken by God from the Book of Genesis until the Book of Revelation is Christ.

People were not able to see God's Word back then. They only heard God speaking His Word to them, and they obeyed His Word.

The People from the beginning obeyed God's Word, which is Christ. Adam and Eve bowed before Christ as the Word of God, even though He was not made flesh yet, and called Christ at that time. Even satan and all his angels obeyed God's Word before they were cast out of Heaven.

Jesus was never called by His Name, Jesus Christ, back then. He was the Word of God. But since God made His Word flesh, He called Him Jesus Christ.

However, right after the Word of God was made flesh, people could now see the Word that God was speaking to Moses, all the prophets, and everyone else from the beginning.

The Lord Jesus Christ said in John 8:56, Your father Abraham rejoiced to see my day: and he saw it and was glad.

The most impossible mystery that the World has been waiting on, which is the Word that God speaks when communicating to mankind; the Word He spoke to create the universe; that Word was made flesh and seen by many.

That Word died for all mankind to rescue them from their sins and bring them back to God the Father.

Anyone who is not serving both God the Father and Christ Jesus is really misled because Christ as the Word of God is Who they ought to obey in order to come to God.

Jesus tells us in John 14:6 that no one comes to the Father but through Him. Why? Because there is no way you will come to God without having a strong relationship with His Word, Christ Jesus.

Let's say you believe that the Torah is the Word of God and also the Bible and still don't believe in Christ, then you don't believe in what the Torah or Bible says.

John 5:39-40, 46-47 says,

> *You study the Scriptures diligently because you think that in them you have eternal life. These are the very Scriptures that testify about me,*
>
> *yet you refuse to come to me to have life.*
>
> *If you believed Moses, you would believe me, for he wrote about me.*
>
> *But since you do not believe what he wrote, how are you going to believe what I say?"*

Jesus Christ made it clear that if they believed what Moses wrote, then they would believe in Him.

That means they didn't believe what Moses wrote because what Moses wrote was the Word of God (the commandments of God), many years before the Word of God was made flesh and Named Jesus Christ.

Moses and all the other prophets were talking about the invisible Word of God to the People, until God made His invisible Word visible. Then, people were able to see God's Word with their eyes.

Let me ask you something simple: How can someone listen to you without you talking to them so they can hear what you tell them?

It's the same with God. For you to listen to God and serve Him, He needs to speak His Word to you, so you can hear what He tells you to do and obey Him.

Whenever God speaks, He always speaks His Word (Jesus Christ) out, so you will always obey Jesus Christ, because Jesus Christ is the Word of God.

Stay Where You Are!

Now let me explain how God told me to stay where I am.

There was a time when I was kind of confused and didn't know which path to take. I had two brothers-in-law, one a Muslim, and the other a Jehovah's Witness. They were both trying to convince me to join them. I'd gotten to a point where I didn't know what to do.

I used to get embarrassed when they would use

my Bible and challenge me that Jesus Christ is not God, and I never could defend my beliefs because I hadn't yet received the Revelation on Who Christ really is.

They always seemed to be correct, but now I see they were always wrong. And it's not that they did it on purpose, but they simply didn't have any revelation about Who Jesus Christ is, or never heard the truth about Him. I really thank God for revealing Christ to me.

I never used to read the Bible front to back but once I started reading the Bible from Genesis to Revelation a few times, God the Father started to appear to me often and taught me His Word.

Don't get me wrong: it's not because I read my Bible front to back a few times that made God appear to me. Many others have read their Bible way more than I did. God appeared to me because I was already chosen in His plan through Christ the Word.

I encourage all my brethren to always read the Word of God, because this is the only way God the Father can communicate and reveal His Word. Even Christ said He is the Only Way to

God the Father. And that's true, because the Word of God is the Only way to God.

How can you do God's will without doing what His Word teaches? Impossible!

Jesus Christ was right; you cannot go to God without going through His Word, which is Christ Himself.

I remember on February 25, 2013, my brother-in-law who is a Muslim came to my house on the occasion of my son's birthday. He was with another Muslim friend of his. They both were trying to convince me to become a Muslim.

I went and prayed to God that night from my heart. I said to Him, "You know that I don't care about religions. It doesn't matter which assembly you tell me to go, because all I ever want, is to do your will through Christ the Word. I'm not attached to anyone else but You only."

I was ready for an answer from Him on what direction to take. That same night, He came and said to me not to go to any other religion but to stay a Christian.

I can tell you that now, no one on earth can ever

pull me out of Christianity after God confirmed it to me. I would consider the true Church of God as the only perfect thing we have left on earth right after Jesus Christ rose from the dead.

I consider the Church as pure as gold because the Church is the Bride of Christ. By the Church, I do not mean the building but those who believe in Christ the Word, and let Him dwell in them to change them for the glory of the Father.

The Bible never teaches us religion, but rather to do God's will through Christ Jesus.

Fourteen

God Allowed Me To Place My Mom in Heaven

14

> "There is nothing you can do to make God see you as a special person in His eyes; instead, He is the One who will make you look special in His eyes by doing His work in you through His Word."

God Allowed Me To Place My Mom In Heaven

> **Then I said to her, "Mom, I brought you to Heaven, and this room is where God has..."**

Traveling to heaven back and forth a few times was never something I expected myself from God the Father. But just like He said to Moses in Exodus 33:19,

I will cause all My goodness to pass before you, and I will proclaim My name~the LORD~in your presence. I will have mercy on whom I have

mercy, and I will have compassion on whom I have compassion.

There is absolutely nothing we can do on our own to make the Lord happy. It doesn't matter whether we are the nicest people or the most gifted people in the world. I mean, there's nothing we can do.

The great Apostle Paul tells us in Ephesians 2:8, *For it is by grace you have been saved, through faith - and this is not from yourselves, it is the gift of God. Think about this verse and see if we deserve anything from God, if it's not by grace.*

Most of us these days are doing our own works and think it comes from God. It does not matter if any of us has a world full of Churches or more people at our buildings than anyone else in the world, and we think it's God's work.

We could be completely wrong if it's not God Who tells us to do such a thing. And we will pay for that at Judgment Day if we don't repent.

We can't let the devil use God's Temple to do his will instead of doing God's will. We could be traveling preaching the Gospel but if it's still not God's work, then our works will be burnt on

Judgement Day, because it's from our flesh and not from the Lord.

There is nothing you can do to make God see you as a special person in His eyes; instead, He is the One who will make you look special in His eyes by doing His work in you through His Word.

So, for me to be able to take my mother's soul to Heaven was something special to me. I don't take any of God's graces for granted.

I remember during the Covid-19 in 2020, my mother had a few strokes and lost her memory. Before she lost her memory, we always talked about the Lord.

During the Pandemic in 2020, God showed me that I took her soul to Heaven, and when I got there with her, there was that big room where all the saved souls were.

Then I said to her, "Mom, I brought you to Heaven, and this room is where God has all the souls that are saved. You are in God's Hands, and you are saved."

After I left her in that room where I saw many other souls of those who were saved, I walked down the stairs from Heaven all by myself back to earth.

I know Jacob said He saw a ladder from Heaven, but I saw stairs connected from Heaven to earth. And in my opinion, I truly believe that there are stairs that connect from Heaven to earth.

I also believe that Heaven is not that far away from us like we think. In reality, I believe it's because of our sins that Heaven seems to be far. In spirit, I think Heaven is right with us.

God is never far from us; our sins separate us from Him. Let's take a clear example in the Bible: When the army of Pharaoh went after the Israelites in the Red Sea, the Bible tells us that all of their horses were running in one spot and never could catch the people until they all got out of there. Then God destroyed the Egyptians.

We also see in the Book of Acts where Stephen was being stoned to death. He said He saw God sit on His Throne and Christ at His Right Hand.

Do you think with his physical eyes He could ever see God and Christ in Heaven?

Once God opened his spiritual eyes, he was able

to see Heaven right above him, where he could see both God the Father and the Son, Jesus Christ.

I believe there is no such thing as distance when we are in spirit.

I do believe Heaven is not too far away because the LORD says, Heaven is my throne, and the earth is my footstool (Isaiah 66:1).

That shows there is not much of a distance. That's how close Heaven and earth are when you are in spirit.

We can't let the devil use God's Temple to do his will instead of doing God's will.

A Glimpse of Judgment Day

15

"
Well, I can tell you this: I saw God the Father Judging the world. I stood next to His Throne and I saw exactly what Jesus Christ said in Matthew 25:33,...
"

A Glimpse of Judgment Day

Have you ever thought about how judgment day will be, or how it's like?

Well, I've been there before. I went to Heaven on Judgment day. So, I've seen God judging the wicked and unbelievers.

I'm sure you'd want to ask, "Who did you see judging the world? Christ Jesus or God the Father? Some Bible verses say that Jesus Christ will judge the nations, while some say God will judge the world; so then, how many judges will we have?

"And since you went to Heaven on judgment's day, was it both the Father and the Son you saw? Who did you see judging? God the Father or the Lord Jesus Christ?"

Now, according to John 5:22, Jesus said in His own Words, that, *The Father judges no one but has given all judgment to the Son.*

Again, Matthew 25:31-32 says,

but when the Son of Man comes in His glory, and all the angels with Him, then He will sit on His glorious throne. And all the nations will be gathered before Him; and He will separate them from one another, as the shepherd separates the sheep from the goats.

On the other hand, Psalms 9:7,8 says,

But the LORD sits enthroned forever, He has established His throne for judgment. He judges the world with righteousness; He judges the peoples with equity.

Many other verses of Scripture talk about God judging the world. For example, Romans 2:2,3,5 says,

We know that God's judgment on those who do such things is in accordance with truth. Do you imagine, whoever you are, that when you judge those who do such things and yet do them yourself, you will escape the judgment of God? But by your hard and impenitent heart you are storing up wrath for yourself on the day of wrath, when God's righteous judgment will be revealed.

From the above Scriptures, we clearly see that God will be judging the world and Jesus Christ will be judging the world. So, how can we be sure Which of them will be the main Judge? Will there be one or two judges?

Well, I can tell you this: I saw God the Father Judging the world. I stood next to His Throne and I saw exactly what Jesus Christ said in Matthew 25:33, that He shall set the sheep on His Right Hand, but the goats on the Left.

Was that a contradiction?

I know for sure that I saw God the Father sit on His Throne, yet I said I saw exactly what Jesus Christ said in Matthew 25:33.

So, did I see Jesus Christ separating the sheep from the goats?

I will give you a glimpse of this revelation, so you understand Who the Judge is.

God is the only Judge. I fully understand that Jesus Christ said, "My Father judges no one but will give all judgment to the Son."

Yes, that's 100% true and correct. But for God to pass His Judgement so all flesh can hear, He has to speak out His Word. And His Word was made flesh, Who is Jesus Christ.

Before now, no one could see God's Word. He was invisible. They could only hear God's voice. But since His Word has been made flesh, when God the Father speaks, we can see His Word talking to us.

It's not Jesus talking to us as a separate Person from the Father, but the Father Himself talking to us using His Word, Jesus Christ, to give us instructions on how to live for Him.

Now, when someone says they see Jesus Christ speaking to them in their dream, vision, or revelation, it's actually God the Father talking to them, but He allows them to see the Word He is speaking to them.

In the same way, on Judgement Day, God the Father is the only One judging. But since the perfect Word that comes out of His mouth, the perfect Word that He is speaking to judge the world with, was made flesh, Who is Christ Jesus, then we will be able to see Jesus Christ as the perfect Word that comes out of His mouth standing on His Right Hand to judge the nations, to separate the sheep from the goats, and to tell the angels to take the unjust to the lake of fire.

In reality, however, it's God the Father telling the angels to take them to the lake of fire.

In essence, we will be able, not only to hear God's judgment but also see His Word, Jesus Christ, in a Human Form.

I hope this helps you to understand the reality of Who Jesus Christ really is. In my next book, you will learn a lot more about the Deity of the Lord Jesus Christ.

What Else Did I See on Judgment Day?

Well, like I mentioned above, I saw God sit on His Throne and I saw two groups of people just like Jesus Christ described in Matthew 25:33, some on God's Right, and the others on His Left.

Some years ago, my ex-wife's brother, who was a Jehovah's Witness, used to try to convince me to join them. He always told me that Jesus Christ is not God, but a god, and just a man that was created from the beginning before all things.

At that time, I didn't know what to tell him because no one could explain to me the verses he was using to prove that Jesus Christ is not God. I did all the research I could but never found an answer. So, I spent time seeking God.

I spent about 16 hours daily studying the Bible and praying. Within seven (7) months, I read the entire Bible three (3) times (front to back), and the New Testament (Matthew to Revelation) fifteen (15) times.

God saw how much I fell in love with His Word, Jesus Christ, and gave me the privilege of visiting Heaven on Judgment Day. Then He told me that many of the people I saw on His Left are those who call themselves Jehovah's Witnesses.

He said they don't believe in Who Jesus Christ is. They don't believe that God's Word is also God. They don't believe that God's Word is Eternal, the Creator of the universe and all mankind, and Forever Living with God as His perfect Word that Moses and the prophets heard or encountered in the Old Testament.

He said they were all going to the lake of fire. I was shocked when I heard that, and when I woke up in the morning, I was like, 'I can't believe it.'

Ever since then, God has taken me to Heaven more times, to show and teach me more about Who Christ really is.

Eight Supernatural Battles:
When God and Christ Fought for Me

EIGHT SUPERNATURAL BATTLES: WHEN GOD AND CHRIST FOUGHT FOR ME

The great Apostle Paul mentioned in 2Timothy 3:12 that everyone who wants to live a godly life in Christ Jesus will be persecuted.

There are all types of persecutions the devil will bring against you. He will try to persecute you day and night. He never stops going after you as long as you're alive. All he cares about is disconnecting you from the Lord.

But like the Apostle Paul said, What, then, shall we say in response to these things? If God is for us, who can be against us? (Romans 8:31).

During my teachings from the Lord, I was going through so much. As I've stated in earlier chapters, my marriage was broken right at the beginning of my teachings with the Lord. Life was tough for me. I never thought I would make it this far with the Lord.

After my marriage was broken, I was being persecuted in my dreams and other things also happened to me in real life. I never thought they really had anything to do with the Lord. To me, it was normal as a Christian, to be persecuted, just as the great Apostle Paul mentioned.

What I really learned from God is that once He chooses you to do His work, you will automatically be one of the most persecuted persons. The devil will set you up everywhere you go. He will try his very best to make you disappoint God just like Adam and Eve did.

I believe the devil knew something was going to happen because I could tell by the way I was being persecuted.

At first, I thought it had to do with the sins I committed in the past. I thought God was making me pay for them all by permitting the devil to cause me pain, just like He permitted the devil to go after Job, even though he could never touch his soul as God already warned him.

Most of the persecutions I've experienced in my journey with the Lord were mostly in my dreams.

I think the devil attacks you more in your dreams than when you are awake. He attacks your spirit because that's what he wants. He always thinks he can win over you when you are asleep. He attacks your soul when your spirit goes places.

Don't you sometimes see your spirit goes to some places when you are sleeping? Yes, your spirit leaves your body, goes to visit some other places, and comes back when it's time to come back to your body. This is where the devil tries to attack your soul while your spirit is out there walking around.

Sometimes your spirit will fight the devil to try

and get back to your body. Sometimes you can win, or sometimes you might lose. That's why a lot of people might go to sleep and don't wake up in the morning. They most likely get into a fight with a demon, and they lose to them.

Sometimes, if the person has Christ in their life, Christ will definitely rescue their soul from the devil's hands and makes their spirit get back in their body.

Here is what the Apostle Paul tells us about spiritual forces of evil:

Finally, be strong in the Lord and in his mighty power.

Put on the full armor of God, so that you can take your stand against the devil's schemes.

For our struggle is not against flesh and blood, but against the rulers, against the authorities, against the powers of this dark world and against the spiritual forces of evil in the heavenly realms.

Therefore put on the full armor of God, so that when the day of evil comes, you may be able to stand your ground, and after you have done

everything, to stand.
Stand firm then, with the belt of truth buckled around your waist, with the breastplate of righteousness in place,

and with your feet fitted with the readiness that comes from the gospel of peace.

In addition to all this, take up the shield of faith, with which you can extinguish all the flaming arrows of the evil one.

Take the helmet of salvation and the sword of the Spirit, which is the word of God.
Ephesians 6:10

I had a few battles in my dreams. I'm talking about huge battles where I could never get out of any of them by myself. I have listed them below, so you see that spiritual warfare is real while sleeping.

A DEMON ATTACKED ME WHILE WATCHING BASKETBALL IN MY ROOM.

This was like a mystery for me because I had never experienced something ever like this before in my life. That was in the year 2009. I was not a church member at that time. I was one of those young people who was chilling out there.

I would go to the gym every day, sometimes twice a day so I could look good. I would go partying and clubbing, and go on vacations to satisfy my fleshly desire.

But the Lord already had a plan for me. He knew He was making me come back to Him one day, and it didn't take me long to come to Him right after this spiritual battle took place.

As I got back from the gym, I did not even shower yet, I lay on my bed a bit to watch Miami Heat playing.

Suddenly, I heard someone talking to me so loud, saying that was my last night, and that I would never see another night ever again.

I got up and went to the bathroom. I looked at myself in the mirror and slapped both sides of my head to be sure I wasn't sleeping.

I went back to lay on the bed again, and all of a sudden a demon started to fight my spirit. A spirit can fight with another spirit, just like we humans can fight others in the physical body.

So, he grabbed me and I felt like the demon slammed me on the bed, got on top of me, and started choking me. That was all in spirit.

My mouth was full of water, so I couldn't scream. It wasn't the physical water, but in spirit.

I was fighting for my life on the bed but there was nothing I could really do about it. My breath stopped, but there was that very last little breath left before I passed.

God the Father put the Name of Jesus in that last breath. At that instance, two words would be too long to say, and would also be too late for me.

As it were, I was already dead in my physical body, but like two seconds before my spirit completely left the body, my soul yelled, "JESUS!" That was how my soul was released from the demon by God.

The only Word that could save me, the only Name that God gave under heaven to save, the Most Authoritative, and the Most Powerful One that ever existed, the Alpha, the Omega, the First and the Last, the King of all kings, the Creator of all things. And yes, "the only Name I could call on was JESUS."

The Power in the Name of Jesus pushed the demon away from me. And when I came back alive, my physical body awoke.

My mouth was completely empty because there was never water in my physical mouth. It was my spirit mouth that the devil filled with water so I wouldn't be able to call on Jesus, the only Name that saves.

I was so afraid that I didn't want to sleep by myself in the room.

We were four at the apartment. So, I ran upstairs to one of my roommates and explained to him what had just happened to me in my room.

He too didn't want me to sleep in his room with him, because he was scared as well. I remember I went to another roommate and slept on the floor that night.

The Power in the Name of Jesus pushed the demon away from me...

CHRIST JESUS CAME TO DELIVER ME AMONG THOUSANDS OF DEMONS IN MY DREAM

While many people don't believe in dreams, especially when it comes to God or Christ Jesus, I can say that this is when God can communicate with you better, just like He has done for many people from creation until today.

Even God Himself said He speaks to His people in their dreams.

The reason God communicates with you better in your dreams is that when you are sleeping, your spirit can separate itself from your body.

Your spirit can leave your body anytime without your permission. And God can take you, while you're in spirit, wherever He wants to meet with or to talk to you.

Sometimes, your spirit doesn't go back to the body. That's why some people go to bed peacefully and don't wake up the next morning. And that's why we should all be thankful every time we go to sleep and wake up the next morning. No one makes you wake up in the morning but God alone.

This is the same thing for satan the devil. He communicates with his people in their sleep. He tells them what to do when he takes their spirit to the invisible world.

Satan always watches when your spirit leaves your body to go places, then he follows you to see if he can stop it from getting back to your body, especially if you're not one of his people.

Satan will fight your spirit so bad with all of his demons, and when you're facing that situation, only Christ Jesus can save your spirit from satan the destroyer, if you call on His Name. Romans 10:13 says, *For whosoever shall call upon the name of the Lord shall be saved.*

So, when Jesus Christ came to save me among thousands of demons, I was sleeping and I saw in my dream that I was among thousands of demons. They were dressed like an army. They were all in uniform; none of them was different from the other.

They all had the same kind of weapons to destroy me. Then I had nowhere to go, and I thought I was going to die. And they would definitely kill me if it weren't for Christ Jesus.

I saw someone dressed in the same type of uniform as them, and carrying a huge weapon coming toward me at great speed. When I saw Him, I was so afraid. I thought He was coming to shoot me.

But when He got in front of me, He said, "Pierre, don't be afraid. This is Me Jesus Christ. I'm dressed just like them, so they don't recognize Who I am."

I was so happy to see how the Lord came to save me among all those demons. Christ touched me and said, "You are fully protected and nothing will happen to you."

Once Christ showed up to me, the demons didn't react at all, because they saw that Christ was in the same uniform as them. They thought Christ was really one of them. That's why they left me alone with Christ.

I thank God the Father for sending His Holy Word (Christ the Messiah) to come and save me among all those demons. I truly believe 100% that demons exist just like God and His Word, Christ, exist.

The best way you will know that demons really

exist, is when you accept Christ Jesus who is the Word of God the Father in your life. Then you will see how much you are being persecuted days and nights.

Whether you're awake or asleep, you will always be persecuted. But if you are one of satan's, then don't worry, you will never be persecuted until he kills you. He never persecutes his people, unless it's time for him to drink their blood. Then he will kill them.

Other than that, you will be just fine on earth. All those who don't have Christ in their lives are living a good life here on earth, but the moment they die, it's over for them. No one can pray for them to be saved.

Once their spirit is gone from the body, their soul goes to the place that was prepared for them to be tormented forever, for not being obedient to the Word of God.

If you have Christ in your life, you will be persecuted for sure by those around you, such as your co-workers, your neighbors, and your friends. Even your own house will rise against you because of the Word of God in you.

Don't get discouraged, instead be courageous because you are persecuted for Christ, the Holy Word of God.

Always remember that, no matter how close the non-believers are to you, once you start serving the Lord deeply, you could be one of the most hated ones. Most of your old friends will not be as close as they used to.

1John 5:19 says, *We know that we are children of God, and that the whole world is under the control of the evil one.*

THE DEVIL MADE ME SWALLOW A SNAKE WHILE I WAS SLEEPING

There was another time I remembered in one of my dreams that the devil was fighting with me, and he made me swallow a live snake. I can never forget that. I thought I was going to die, but the Lord was with me and didn't let me die.

That dream was supposed to be straight death for me, but the Lord knew that He was going to prepare me for His work, so He was always watching over me, protecting me from my childhood until today.

My mother always told me how God was always with me, and I have always loved God since childhood.

This dream was a while back. I don't really remember all of it, but what I do remember is that I was forced to swallow a snake, and after I swallowed it, I was so scared in the dream.

I remember I had my Bible with me, and God commanded me to eat all the pages from the Bible, and I started to eat them all. I ate the entire Bible just like when God commanded the Prophet Ezekiel to eat the scroll in Ezekiel 3:3.

The way God made me interpret this dream was to tell me all that was coming into my life, including all the persecutions that I've been having for the past couple of years.

That dream was a prophecy to tell me there would be things coming my way, but with the Word of God that is in my life, the Word of God that is made one with me, nothing would happen to me, unless the time had come for me to go.

Now, I understand why I was always reading my Bible so much. I've read it a few times, and that was exactly what the Lord showed me from that dream - eating all the pages of my Bible.

It didn't mean literally I was eating the pages of the Bible. But just like Jesus said to the Pharisees in the Book of John 6:53, *Very truly I tell you, unless you eat the flesh of the Son of Man and drink his blood, you have no life in you.*

Well, I can say that was exactly what I was doing, eating His Flesh and drinking His Blood, meaning I've been eating the Word of God so much until the Word is made One with me.

It's important to let the Word of God dwell in you no matter what you're going through.

I really thank God for making provision for me about 25 years ago. He gave me His Holy Word to be with me, to protect me, and to be One with me.

④

 **JESUS CHRIST CAME DOWN BETWEEN ME AND A HUGE SNAKE THAT ALMOST SWALLOWED ME.**

I remember this was way before my marriage got broken. It was in 2013, even though I didn't know much about the Lord at that level. At least, I was an active member of the Church I attended.

There was that night while I was sleeping, and I was by a big river, then I saw a huge snake, way bigger than an anaconda that we've seen in movies.

I saw a baby boy by the river, and I had no idea where that child came from. I saw that the snake grabbed the child and swallowed him.

I wasn't scared of the snake at all. So, I walked into the river to face it, and got right in front of it. There wasn't too much gap between us.

The snake lifted his head so high above my head. Then it opened its mouth so wide and brought its head down to swallow me.

The snake thought it got me, because it was only the two of us in the river. It was ready to swallow me. The devil probably forgot that "There is therefore no condemnation to them which are in Christ Jesus, who walk not after the flesh, but after the Spirit".

The snake's mouth was so close, about three seconds away from swallowing me. Then I saw Christ Jesus descend between the two of us. Christ was now facing the snake, and I was behind Him. Then Christ pounded on His left chest with His Right Hand three times, and pointed His finger at the snake.

He said to the snake, "You surely will persecute my servant. You will make a lot of things happen to his life. You will make him miserable. But one thing I can tell you, you will never be able to touch his soul." The snake turned around and left.

When I woke up in the morning, I thanked God for sending His Word (Christ) to rescue me. Other than that, I wouldn't make it in the morning.

That is why it is so important to pray before we go to sleep every night. Even if you cannot pray because you are so tired, try to say something to God even in five seconds. He will understand.

(5)

I TORE A BIG SNAKE IN A VISION AS I LAY DOWN ON MY COUCH AT MY HOUSE.

This was in 2015 right after my ex-wife left me. That was when I had a lot of persecutions going on. The devil tried his best and everything he could do to destroy me, but the Lord was always with me and never forsook me as He promised us.

One of the last things the devil will do to destroy you is to come to you like a snake. As you already know from the Bible, he is the old serpent. That old serpent appeared to me twice.

When his messengers can't do anything to you, then the serpent will come. This is the last stage of your persecutions.

If for any reason that snake kills you in your visions or dreams, you're so done unless it's God that let it happen so He can show you His Mighty power.

Snakes are very bad in dreams or visions.

There was that evening I lay down on my couch, and I knew I was not sleeping. My eyes were simply closed, but God wanted to show me in what form satan comes to persecute me. He opened my spiritual eyes so I could see what was going on.

As I lay down, I saw a huge yellow and black snake pass right in from of me. I reached down from the couch and put my hands on the snake, and all I was saying was, "In the Name of Jesus, in the Name of Jesus," and repeated it over and over.

At the same time, I was trying to tear it apart or split it into two pieces because I grabbed it from the head and tail. I was pulling it so hard, but nothing happened. As I opened my eyes, I still felt I was pulling it to split it into pieces.

I could say it was such a great victory that God gave me. The snake came to my house in spirit form, believing I would not see it.

It probably thought it would come live at my house. But thanks to the Lord for allowing me to see it and tear it apart with the power in the Name of Jesus.

 ## SATAN TOOK ME TO THE INVISIBLE WORLD AND FORCED ME TO DRINK POISON TO KILL ME.

We all know how powerful satan is, but Our God the Father is the Creator of all things. He is the Almighty God, the God that no one can stop from doing whatever He wants to do.

Compared to God the Father, satan has no power at all. It was all given to him by the Father after he was created as one of God's angels. But that doesn't mean he's not powerful compared to mankind.

The only way we, as mankind, are more powerful than him, is only when we have Jesus Christ as the Word of God the Father living in us. Other than that, there is nothing we can do to fight this creature because power was given to him by the Father.

As you can see, the devil is so powerful, he tempts people to sin against God. He even turns their back against their Creator and makes them serve the creature instead.

We saw how the devil tried to mislead Jesus

Christ in the wilderness.

Matthew 4:5 says, *Then the devil took Him up into the holy city, set Him on the pinnacle of the temple, and said to Him, "If You are the Son of God, throw Yourself down."*

That shows you how powerful satan is, but one thing we must remember, in the Book of Philippians 2:7 the great Apostle Paul tells us, *but Christ emptied Himself by taking the form of a bond-servant and being born in the likeness of men.*

If Christ didn't empty Himself to come to earth, there is no way the devil could lead Him anywhere. God knew if He let His Word, Christ, come to earth with all His power, nothing could stop Christ on earth. So, God the Father took all His power away from His Word, which is Christ.

After the Word of God accomplished everything God desired Him to do, which was to come to die for our sins, the Word of God got all His power back from the Father right after He got resurrected from the dead.

Matthew 28:18 says, *And Jesus came and spake unto them, saying, All power is given unto me in heaven and in earth.*

I hope you understand the reason why the devil was able to tempt Christ in the wilderness.

As you can see, the devil has all the mighty power to tempt anyone on this earth, but he got no power at all to make you do anything that you don't want to do, unless you agree with him while you're being tempted. Only then will he have the power to make you do the things that he wants you to do.

We have millions of examples every single day, where the devil tempts the entire world. Once they agree with him, he takes control over them, to live in them, and to make their body his temple to use whenever he decides to do whatever he wants, to satisfy his desire.

Therefore, he was tempting Christ to see if Christ could agree with him. We saw the answer Christ gave him, and he left Him.

The reason why I explained all these, is to make sure that we are aware of satan's power when we are empty. The only thing that can make us way more powerful than the devil, is to have Christ Jesus in our lives. That is, to follow the Word of

God, to walk by the Word of God, and to live by the Word of God. Without the Word of God, we are nothing.

In John 15:5, Jesus Christ tells us, *I am the vine; you are the branches. Whoever abides in me and I in him, he it is that bears much fruit, for apart from me you can do nothing.*

A great example we have in the Bible is Judas. He got tempted with money and agreed with the devil to hand Christ to them.

I remember that night when I was sleeping, and the devil took my spirit to the invisible World. They tied both of my hands, and there were many demons gathered.

The place where they took me was underneath the earth. It's another world where they take many people to go and sacrifice.

They were all forcing me to drink poison, but I refused. They came to open my mouth and pour the poison inside of me. Then I heard them say, "Let's watch him die now."

I rather felt so strong on the inside after drinking the poison. It seemed like they gave me some great protein to drink, because that's how Christ made me feel.

I told them, "Even though all of you forced me to drink the poison, I will not die because the Lord Christ is with me."

Mark 16:18 says, *They shall take up serpents; and if they drink any deadly thing, it shall not hurt them; they shall lay hands on the sick, and they shall recover.*

When I was among them in the invisible world, I was being so mean to them. I had such confidence to talk back to them after I drank the poison. I was not afraid of them at all, because the Lord was with me.

Also, God the Father promised us in Psalms 91:4-16,

> *He will cover you with his feathers, and under his wings you will find refuge; his faithfulness will be your shield and rampart.*

> *You will not fear the terror of night, nor the arrow that flies by day,*

> *nor the pestilence that stalks in the darkness, nor the plague that destroys at midday.*

A thousand may fall at your side, ten thousand at your right hand, but it will not come near you.

You will only observe with your eyes and see the punishment of the wicked.

If you make the Most High your dwelling-- even the LORD, who is my refuge--

then no harm will befall you, no disaster will come near your tent.

For he will command his angels concerning you to guard you in all your ways;

they will lift you up in their hands, so that you will not strike your foot against a stone.

You will tread upon the lion and the cobra; you will trample the great lion and the serpent.

"Because he loves me," says the LORD, "I will rescue him; I will protect him, for he acknowledges my name.

He will call upon me, and I will answer him; I will be with him in trouble, I will deliver him and honor him.

With long life will I satisfy him and show him my salvation."

All these promises are for those who are in Christ Jesus. Once you're in Christ, you have 100% protection from God.

The good thing I love about God is that you can't fake Him. If you are truly in Christ, you're protected, and nothing from the devil can happen to you, unless He allows it to happen to you for His own glory.

7

I SAW A DEMON FACE-TO-FACE IN REAL LIFE AFTER CALLING THE NAME OF JESUS CHRIST.

How possible is it for anyone to see a demon face-to-face? I'm not talking about visions or dreams.

When Jesus Christ talked to the demons, they talked back to Him. So, Jesus Christ didn't only see the people who had the demons in them talking to Him, He also saw the demons and cast them out.

For example, in Luke 8:2, Jesus cast out seven demons out of Mary Magdalene.

Also, Matthew chapter 8:28-34 tells us,

> *And when He came to the other side into the country of the Gadarenes, two demon-possessed men confronted Him as they were coming out of the tombs. They were so extremely violent that no one could pass by that way.*
>
> *And they cried out, saying, "What business do You have with us, Son of God? Have You come here to torment us before the time?"*
>
> *Now there was a herd of many pigs feeding at a distance from them.*
>
> *And the demons begged Him, saying, "If You are going to cast us out, send us into the herd of pigs."*
>
> *And He said to them, "Go!" And they came out and went into the pigs; and behold, the whole herd rushed down the steep bank into the sea and drowned in the waters.*

The demons were talking to Christ through the man who was possessed. And like I said, Christ saw the demons. The demons are spirits. The people who were possessed by the demons had no idea Who Christ was, but the demons in them knew Who Christ was.

There were many other people in the Bible that God allowed to see spirits in real life.

2 Kings 6:15-18 tells us,

> *When the servant of the man of God got up and went out early in the morning, an army with horses and chariots had surrounded the city. So he asked Elisha, "Oh, my master, what are we to do?"*
>
> *"Don't be afraid," the prophet answered. "Those who are with us are more than those who are with them."*
>
> *And Elisha prayed, "Open his eyes, LORD, so that he may see." Then the LORD opened the servant's eyes, and he looked and saw the hills full of horses and chariots of fire all around Elisha.*

This was not a vision or dream. The great Prophet Elisha saw the horses, but his servant didn't see them yet. The great prophet Elisha prayed to God the Father to open his servant's eyes so he could see that the Lord was with them.

God allowed His servants' eyes to be opened so they could see the invisible. This is exactly what I experienced when God opened my eyes to see a demon that day.

I remember it was right after I finished reading my Bible. It was around 2 AM and I turned off the light. I felt something was not right, but I didn't see anything yet. Suddenly, spiritual warfare started.

Every time the demon hit me, I could feel it in my spirit but when I punched in the direction I was getting punched from, I didn't feel that I hit anything, because the demon was invisible.

The demon punched me again. Then right before I punched back, I said, "in the Name of Jesus", and punched. Suddenly, I saw a lady appear before me.

The Name of Jesus made the demon visible, so I could see who I was fighting. I grabbed her from her t-shirt with the authority of the Lord, and I tore it apart.

I saw that she was wearing a brassiere. I grabbed her from it, and I said, "in the Name of Jesus," and punched her on her left breast so hard with the power of Jesus Christ. Then she was gone.

I said to myself, "What!" Was that real? because I know I wasn't sleeping. I wasn't in any vision, and a demon came to attack me like that. I was shocked and didn't want to sleep.

I was so afraid at that time because I met demons in my dreams many times. I fought them many times in the past. But to be able to see one appear to me face-to-face in real life was insane to me.

Even though I know it was the power that is in the Name of Jesus Christ that transformed the demon and made her visible, it was still a shock to me.

I remember that song that says, "There is power, power in the Name of the Lord." And the great Apostle Paul also mentioned in many passages in the Bible about the power that is in the Name of Jesus Christ.

We also know that there is no condemnation for those who are in Christ Jesus. No matter how the demons come to attack you, once you are in the Lord Christ, nothing can come by your house to hurt you or your family members.

I remember back in 2012, a year after my son was born, satan came and said to me in a dream, "I did everything I could to take you down, but I can't do anything to you. But what about your son? Can I take him?"

I said to him, "The same way you can't do anything to me, it's the same way you can't do anything to my son."

Then He said to me, "Okay, you're right. But before I go, can we make peace by shaking hands? Can you shake my hands?"

He stretched his right hand to me, and I said to him, "Why would I shake your hand when I'm not your friend? I only shake hands with my friends."

I'm sure if I did shake his hand, that would mean I agreed to make peace with him. But the Spirit of the Lord was in me to make sure nothing like that happened.

(8) GOD THE FATHER AND JESUS CHRIST CAME TO RESCUE ME AMONG MILLIONS OF DEMONS.

Well, I have been in many spiritual battles in the past. But this spiritual battle was not like any other spiritual battles I've had in the past.

We saw especially in the Old Testament when God fought a lot for His people. He stood to fight for them all and promised He would always be there to make sure they had victory in all their battles.

It's the same for your spiritual battles. If you are in the Lord, He fights all your battles.

As I look through Scriptures from Genesis to Revelation, I can say it's more likely that the battles in the Old Testament were more physical. Then, during the time Christ was on earth, we saw how it changed from physical battles to spiritual warfare.

We can see in the New Testament how Jesus Christ cast out demons from several people.

Also, the disciples faced many spiritual battles when they went out to preach during Christ's time, as well as after He was raised from the dead.

My Experience

While I was sleeping, I saw myself in the midst of millions of demons. I could say it looked like the earth was full of demons.

I had nowhere to escape, and I thought that would be my end. But thanks to God the Father and Christ the Son who came from Heaven to fight for me.

I remember when I was among the demons, I was not scared at all. I truly believe that God took away such fears. As I lifted my eyes to Heaven, I saw Jesus Christ and God the Father coming down right in front of me while I was still among all the demons.

I saw that God the Father was standing on the right, and Christ on the left. God the Father stretched His left Hand to Christ, and Christ grabbed His Hand.

As they held their hands together, God said to me, "After today, you will never see demons bothering you like this anymore."

While they still held Hands, God the Father went all the way to the ends of the earth on the Northside, and Christ went all the way to the Southside. Then they both ran over all the demons on the whole earth.

After that, I only saw the three of us left. As I looked on the ground, I didn't see anything, not even a tiny piece of the demons left.

Then I looked up to God and asked, "Where are all the demons that were all around me?"

And God the Father said to me, "Remember I just told you from now on, you will not see demons come to bother you anymore."

I was very happy and felt protected by God after He said that to me.

This is what God can do for His people. God will deliver you from all evil battles. Nothing should happen to you if you have faith in the Lord.

I can tell you that ever since then, I've never seen myself in any spiritual warfare in my dreams or visions because God the Father promised me that I would never see any demons come to bother me ever again.

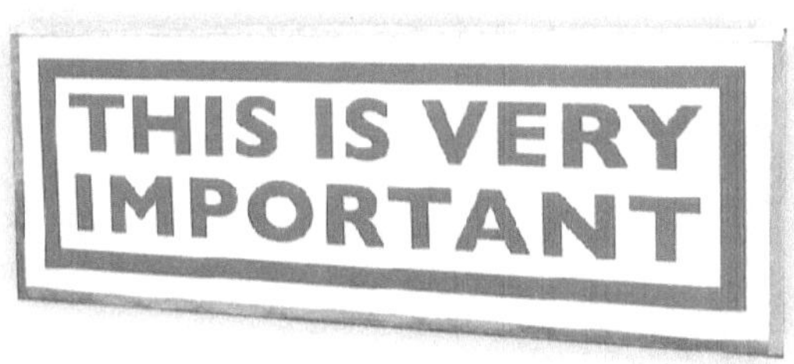

Beloved, you need to surrender your life to the Lordship of Jesus Christ by accepting His sacrificial death on Calvary for you or you need to re-dedicate your life to Jesus Christ.

Pray this prayer with me:

> Lord Jesus, I come before You today to surrender my life completely to you. I have lived a self-centred life that is far separated from God, I have had priorities that are not eternity-centred, I have always lived in rebellion, disobedience and sin up till now.
>
> Lord, I am sorry for the way that I have lived and I ask for your forgiveness and mercy. Lord, please cleanse my sins by your blood and take your place of leadership and rulership in my life.
>
> Fill my heart Lord with the right desires and

priorities. Deliver me from the vanity and fantasies of this world.

Give me the grace to say no to sin and compromise. Give me the grace to live in righteousness and represent you well in my world.

Help me to escape the tragedy of eternity in hell. Help me Lord to make heaven at the end of my journey on earth.

Help me Lord to live both in the consciousness of your presence and of eternity.

Continuously reveal to me everything that would make me unworthy of Heaven.

Thank you Lord for hearing and answering me in Jesus' Name I pray, Amen.

If you have prayed this prayer, please do the following:

1. Send us your name, phone number, and contact address by email: Pnoramebooks@hitaj.org or by phone: +1(561)410-6536.

2. Become serious with God by identifying with a

righteousness and eternity-conscious church.

3. Study your Bible daily to receive a word from God.

4. Speak to God daily in prayer and let Him know your feelings and challenges.

5. Disconnect from every wrong association. Don't follow them to hell if they won't follow you to Heaven.

6. Speak to others about God. Share your testimony of transformed life. Be instrumental in assisting someone to escape hell.

7. Repent promptly. Do not sleep over unconfessed sins. Apply the blood over your soul for cleansing continuously. Live eternity ready.

The Lord bless you.

Index

A

able, 36, 43, 55, 67, 77, 87,94, 103-105, 116, 118-119, 132, 142, 144, 153-154, 163, 171, 175, 184, 189, 197
Abraham, 21, 90, 143
accord, 21
Adam, 34, 86-91, 96, 142, 169
adultery, 20
Adventist, 27
Advocate, 20
affair, 12, 82
Almighty, 114, 131-132, 187
Alpha, 174
altar, 114
America, 6
anaconda, 183
ancestors, 43
angels, 20, 41, 43-44, 86, 116-117, 142, 160, 163, 187, 192
Apostle, 13, 20, 35, 43, 65,71, 75-77, 88, 97-98, 115,130-131, 141, 152, 168-169, 171, 188, 197
Appendix, 167-168
armor, 171
Arms, 78

army, 97, 154, 177, 195
assembly, 147
association, 205
attack, 73, 170, 197-198
attention, 105
attitude, 74
authority, 196

B

baby, 183
bank, 194
baptism, 43-44
BASKETBALL, 172
bathroom, 173
battle, 89, 173, 199
bed, 77-78, 134, 173-174,176
bedroom, 124
beliefs, 21, 146
Bible, 6, 43, 63, 79, 87, 96,104, 115, 130, 139-140,143-144, 146, 148, 154,160, 164, 181-182, 185,190, 195-197, 205
bless, 81, 205
blessing, 107
blood, 73, 171, 179, 182, 203, 205
body, 34, 64, 77, 86, 88-92,115, 170-171, 174-177, 179, 189

Index

Index

Index

Index

war, 98
warfare, 99, 172, 196, 199, 201
watch, 74, 173, 190
water, 43-44, 174-175
weapons, 98, 177
weeds, 61, 81
weights, 55
wheat, 61, 81
wicked, 28, 34, 73, 86, 97, 159, 192
wife, 11-13, 25-28, 34-36, 62, 72-73, 95, 164, 185
wilderness, 66, 80, 188-189
win, 170-171
wings, 114, 191
wisdom, 96, 124
Witness, 145, 164
wonder, 72
world, 79, 86, 90, 98, 152, 160-161, 163, 171, 177, 180, 189-191, 204
worry, 64, 116, 134, 179
worship, 20, 49-50, 140
worthy, 43
wound, 26
wrath, 161

yoke, 67
young, 173

Y

YHWH, 18-20